D0323747

BREAKFAST WITH FRED

FRED SMITH, SR.
MENTOR TO A GENERATION OF LEADERS

Regal
From Gospel Light
Ventura, California, U.S.A.

Published by Regal Books
From Gospel Light
Ventura, California, U.S.A.

Library of Congress Cataloging-in-Publication Data
Smith, Fred, 1915-
Breakfast with Fred / Fred Smith, Sr.
p. cm.
ISBN 978-0-8307-4476-3 (hard cover)
1. Christian life. I. Title.
BV4510.3.S65 2007
248.4—dc22

2007014068

1 2 3 4 5 6 7 8 9 10 / 10 09 08 07

To all the friends of breakfastwithfred.com
who daily encourage us to expand the reach,
deepen the impact and preserve the work.

CONTENTS

ACKNOWLEDGMENTS

Canadian psychiatrist Dr. Hans Selye regarded gratitude as the healthiest of all emotions. With enormously healthy hearts, we say thank you to those who supported this project from the outset. An idea is only a mental construct until someone believes in it and makes it real. With the help of competent advisors, it comes to you as a warm delicacy, not just a half-baked concept. We offer profound appreciation to the following:

The 52 friends and family who entertained the question: How would you apply Fred's words in a way to help others? Their enthusiastic, diligent responses form the backbone of this timely and timeless wisdom book.

Leslie Nunn Reed, literary agent and friend, who saw a book when all we offered were abstractions. Her perseverance, insight and commitment began the process.

Steven Lawson, senior editor at Regal Books, who skillfully and diplomatically pointed out holes and translated them into a whole. His heart for excellence moved this project. His poise and candor kept us operating at "highest and best."

Kim Bangs, at Regal Books, who became part of the BWF community as she encouraged us all.

James Pevehouse, BWF associate and Dallas Seminary graduate, whose friendship, encouragement, calmness and knowledge of Scripture made this project fun on even the most stressful days.

The Saturday morning "Fred in the Bed" group, who primed the pump.

The too-many-to-name group who prodded, probed and prayed through countless hours of preparation.

Psalm 115:1 ultimately sums up all acknowledgments: "Not to us, O Lord, not to us! But to your name bring honor, for the sake of your loyal love and faithfulness."

BILLY GRAHAM

MONTREAT, NORTH CAROLINA 28757

July 17, 2006

Dear Fred,

I have heard that you are not well, but are thinking positively as a result of your lifelong strong faith in Christ.

I have thought of you so many times and thanked God for the witness that you have always given wherever you were. What an inspiration and encouragement you were to so many thousands.

I have so many memories of our to times together. Be assured of my Christian love and appreciation for your friendship.

Billy

Billy Graham

SPECIAL INTRODUCTION

Jeff Horch

It was my turn to sit and watch. The clock in the partially dark hospital room read 2:33 A.M. The sound of liquid medicine dripped quietly like a small fountain as the drops flowed into the elderly man sleeping in the bed a few feet from me. His snoring was peaceful and stable. His face was unshaven. He slept with his mouth just a bit open, like elderly men often do. He looked weak and old, but in fact he was quite strong. And when it came to dying, he was probably too strong and too defiant to passively accept the weakening of his body. He was prepared to die, but he had spent too much of his life developing disciplines of perseverance to simply give up. That is who he is. And as I stared at him, I also saw a glimpse of who I am and who I want to be.

Seeing my grandfather near death, I was reminded not of a man who was dying but of a man who is full of hope. Not *was* but *is* full of hope, even throughout the pain and suffering.

He didn't die that night. And I still see a man of hope. I think you will, too.

As his health has deteriorated over the past few years, he has taught me much in my study of his character. It is easy for someone to exude joy and hope amid good health and physical blessing, but to see those same qualities thrive during suffering means a person has been deeply rooted through a lifetime of faith and discipline. For my grandfather, his faith comes from a secure hope in who his Savior is, and his discipline comes from his having been a good steward of the talents his Creator has given.

It is often said it's not how you start but how you finish that counts. I believe my grandfather is finishing well. He is not a saint nor is he a perfect man, but he is one who lives with a very clear and real grasp of the eternal. He knows this is not his home. And as he has endured the gradual deterioration of his earthly body, he continues to be a compass for many still walking this journey.

In his mid-20s, he decided his life motto would be to "stretch others." His desire has been to help people fully use their God-given gifts and talents. To see him in his early 90s, often in pain, still stretching others reveals to me that the words he lives by are more than a motto—they are the very core of who he is.

Now in my mid-30s, I am challenged in my own attitudes and choices by seeing my grandfather face the end of his life with grace and a sense of peace. I am not naïve enough to think he is simply a cherubic character in a Norman Rockwell painting—I know his humanity. But I also know that he is a man steeped in God's grace, desiring to be used until his very last breath. When he had to give up his freedom and mobility, he could have gotten bitter, but he chose to adapt. At this moment his is still choosing to submit to God's working through him in this new time of life.

I firmly believe this book will give readers of all ages an opportunity to find in Grandfather and his friends thoughts that mentor and strengthen. These are apt words for us as we face life's question marks. They give us insight that only lives of integrity can produce. They mark a path for those of us still learning. Their words point out a direction so that we, too, may finish well.

NOTE FROM THE EDITOR

Brenda A. Smith

We asked, "If we put together a book on Dad's thoughts over 90 years, what would you want to know?"

The replies began time after time with these words: "When I had breakfast with Fred, he said . . ." Those early morning meetings provided mentoring, friendship and thoughtful discussions. Several sent pages of "Fred Notes" taken during years of breakfasts. A definite theme emerged!

In 2002, Dad's health deteriorated seriously. Physically compromised and with a life expectancy of only three to four months, Dad shelved the book idea. So a new idea, developed by Jeff Horch, took shape: a website named www.breakfast withfred.com. The BWF Project, Inc., a nonprofit corporation, sponsors the online archive. We organize and relevantly communicate the lifework and wisdom of Fred Smith, Sr. We are committed to expanding his reach, deepening his impact and preserving his work.

It is now 2006 and Dad has beaten all the odds—and probably the odds-makers! The website now reaches men and women who desire to learn decision-making skills, leadership techniques and communication tips, as well as those seeking to enrich their family life.

Emerson's question to Thoreau, "What has become clearer since last we met?" spurred Dad to share his thoughts via an email bulletin, "Fred's Weekly Thought." Each one gives the subscribers insight into his "crooked thinking on the straight and narrow." The BWF community, stretched and blessed by his wisdom, is now a global fellowship.

This wisdom book is a collection of 52 weekly thoughts joined by thoughtful responses from 52 good friends. You'll read Dad's "conversations" with men such as Zig Ziglar, John Maxwell, Pat Williams and Charlie "Tremendous" Jones—men who call Dad "mentor." His wisdom and principle-based approach to life enable readers to grasp life with a stronger hold. Men and women worldwide will now be able to "breakfast with Fred" and grow in faith, understanding and competence.

Brenda A. Smith
President, BWF Project, Inc.

Fred and Brenda

BREAKFAST WITH FRED

Dear Reader,

Now, at nearly 92, I still enjoy great conversation and great ideas—the two usually go together well.

The www.breakfastwithfred.com weekly thought is my current method of answering the question, "What's on your mind, Fred?" I find it fascinating to know that each week thousands of people read what rolls around in my head (usually in the wee hours of the morning when I can't sleep).

Having 52 long-time friends and family members provide an application for my thoughts is both humbling and invigorating. It allows me to introduce you to them, share my thinking and open the door to wonderful conversation.

Stretching and blessing is my prayer for you.

With kindest personal regards,

Fred Smith

1

EFFECTIVE SELF-MANAGEMENT

Fred's Observation

The hardest person on any executive's team to supervise is himself. He soon recognizes that "my problem is me."

If many people took the energy and intelligence they spend devising ways to avoid work and applied it toward building a work plan, they would be highly successful. One of the most important executive disciplines is cutting off escapes from effective work. Sadly, there are executives who are strategic about accomplishment avoidance. For example, a great many people study their jobs rather than work at them. Most people already know considerably more than they are actually using in the workplace. Education is not the problem—disciplined motivation is.

Another escape for most people is activity. They have not learned "results are the only excuse for activity." Many people feel at day's end that they are satisfied with their efforts when in fact they have just been busy. They are the chief of their local fire department: putting out flames but never constructing buildings. They are on the run but never getting anywhere productive. Too many executives eat, belch and run—like fire trucks with dirty engines. Little boys make lots of noise playing firemen, but grown executives need to put down the helmets.

In order to accomplish anything, you must have a definite goal. Unless you can write it down, it isn't definite or specific. My mentor Maxey Jarman taught me that aimless verbal wandering has no power. Only when I put the goal on paper does it take shape. Until it is formed, it may be a direction—but it isn't a goal. A ship with a lot of steam doesn't get to port unless it stays on course.

Once the goal has been set, it must be pursued with a burning desire. The desire must be maintained and sustained with discipline.

Reflection: John Maxwell

Author and Speaker
Founder, INJOY Stewardship Services and EQUIP

Fred is so right. For many people, if they could kick the person responsible for all their problems, they wouldn't be able to sit down for a week!

To succeed in life, you must get out of your own way. Doing that requires two things. They sound so simple, yet many people fail to master them. They are (1) doing what's best and (2) avoiding the rest.

For many years, I have used three concepts along with three simple questions to help people determine what's holding them back—and then move forward.

1. *Requirement: What Must I Do?* In every job, there are things that you alone must do—they cannot be delegated. If I accept one of the many speaking invitations I receive, I need to show up and speak. I can delegate many other things, such as getting information about the event and making the travel arrangements, but when the audience is there,

I'm the only one who can step onto the stage and deliver the message. If you're an employee, then your boss determines what is required of you. If you're a CEO, the board of directors does. Think about your job, and list the tasks that you alone *must* do.

2. *Return: What Brings the Greatest Results?* What can you do better than anyone else? In what areas do you have the golden touch? Add your items of greatest return to your list.

3. *Reward: What Gives the Most Satisfaction?* Certain activities make a person's heart sing. What are yours? What could you do every day, even if you never got paid for it? Add those things to your list.

Avoid anything that falls outside these three areas. Dump them if you can; delegate them if you must. Ideally, your goal should be to make these three areas—requirement, return and reward—overlap as much as possible. That's working in your strength zone. If you can get to where these three threads come together in your life, you'll be like Thomas Edison, who said, "I never did a day's work in my life; it was all fun."

Three Questions to Think About

1. How do I make sure that I have goals, not just directions?
2. What will it take for me to "get out of my own way"?
3. Do I ever get busy, but not productive?

One Line to Remember

The hardest person on any executive's team to supervise is himself. . . . my problem is me.

Scripture to Hide in Your Heart

In all hard work there is profit, but merely talking about it only brings poverty (Proverbs 14:23).

2

VICTORY THROUGH VISION

Fred's Observation

David Rockefeller was once quoted as saying, "The number one function of the top executive is to establish the purpose of the organization." Like the hub of the wheel, everything else grows out of this priority. Until the vision is established, trouble is ahead. Scripture says, "Where there is no vision, the people perish" (see Proverbs 29:18). The *New American Standard Bible* focuses on the way they perish: "Where there is no vision, the people are unrestrained." To be restrained, to be concentrated in purpose, is essential to accomplishment, and that is why the leader must define why the organization exists.

A leader must personify the vision and be dedicated to it personally. As they seek to maintain the vision, leaders must keep in mind these essentials:

1. Define the vision specifically. Leaders disperse the fog.

2. Express it so that other people understand it. Lingo without logic simply confuses and doesn't galvanize.

3. Get both organizational and personal acceptance of the vision. Nodding heads without knowing hearts keep the motors idling.

4. Repeat the purpose over and over. The Old Testament patriarchs set up stones of remembrance to remind the people of their story (see Joshua 4:5-7). My wife, Mary Alice, always sent the children out the door with the following: "Remember who you are, where you are from and what you represent." She kept their purpose "ever before them."

When you have a clear vision, you view everything in its light. A vision is a filter and a grid through which all activity flows. You come to see the need for a vision broad enough that everything you do can be tied to it. The focused vision will both include and exclude. Despite the work that it takes to craft an effective vision, it is a far better alternative to perishing.

Reflection: Pat Williams
Senior Vice President, Orlando Magic Basketball Club
Author and Motivational Speaker

When Fred talks about vision, I listen . . . and so do many others. We all need mentors, and Fred in his quiet way is a mentor to the world. He is a lifelong learner and loves to pass it along. He is a man of vision and courage. He is a student of people and events. I like to say that every time I speak, I want to change the world. Fred Smith has changed *my* world.

In my book *The Paradox of Power*, I define vision as the ability to see farther than the eye can see and the ability to see what isn't there. Only by seeing what is not there can you bring something new, creative and exciting into existence. I am convinced that vision empowers, clarifies, enthuses, involves, motivates and focuses leaders.

Part of vision is understanding the situation and speaking truth. A good friend of mine was going through a difficult, nasty divorce. It was causing him great consternation. I spoke with Fred about it and he had a simple word: "Doesn't she [my friend's wife] realize that she is making a junkyard out of her old age?" Powerful wisdom. Powerful leadership. Powerful vision.

As a leader of men, I want to cast a vision of character, insatiable curiosity and victory. Fred's comments about focus hit home every time for me. Focus and purpose allow the great passions of our lives to become real. I read a recent study showing that we can operate without passion for about two weeks, but then we implode. Yet passion without vision is merely an empty wish.

Catch the vision. Study what Fred Smith has to say. Learn that we never outgrow our need for wise counsel. Then lead with character, passion and purpose. And plan to win.

Three Questions to Think About

1. How clear is my vision?
2. What am I seeing that inspires confidence in others?
3. How do I personify my vision?

One Line to Remember

When you have a clear vision, you view everything in its light.

Scripture to Hide in Your Heart

When there is no prophetic vision, the people cast off restraint, but the one who keeps the law, blessed is he! (Proverbs 29:18).

3

THE LISTENING LEADER

Fred's Observation

Every leader spends a good part of the day communicating with others. A great many books have been written on techniques of good communication, but the real problem is the spirit, not the technique. Attitude is often the barrier. Almost any two people who want to can talk together. The emphasis on open lines of communication hides a deeper problem. Often people who are unable to communicate find that they are hindered by their desire to impress, not express.

Motivation largely depends on communication, and the difference between a poor team and a good one is generally selection and organization. The difference between a good team and a great one is motivation. Any organization with the ability to get to good can move to great with the proper motivation. And nothing motivates quite like effective communication.

Most leaders are adequate talkers, but inadequate listeners. The ability to listen creatively and positively depends on the leader's ability to listen on four levels: (1) the meaning of the words, (2) the choice of words, (3) the sounds of the words, and (4) the sight of the words. Most people listen negatively, which is simply keeping silent or reloading while the other is shooting. Positive listening guides the talker both in the giving of facts and a display of emotion that permit the listener to evaluate on more than a surface level.

Communication is mistakenly confused with agreement. I often hear people say that all problems would be solved if we really heard and understood each other. Not so! In fact, if we really understood what the other truly was saying, we might have increased disagreement. We talk around subjects in order to avoid points of disagreement. Hearing and understanding are critical to communication but not synonymous with agreement and concord.

Listen to hear. Speak to be understood.

Reflection: Zig Ziglar

Nationally Acclaimed Author, Motivational Speaker and Trainer

The insights of Fred Smith have influenced me personally and professionally for many years now, and I'm honored to respond to his ideas on motivation and communication.

Motivation cannot occur without prior communication. Communication will not be achieved without attentive listening, and the way we listen affects what we think we have heard. Convoluted? Maybe, but try skipping any of the steps that lead to true performance and you'll quickly discover how tightly woven hearing and understanding are to motivation and achievement.

A true leader desires what is best for his or her company *and* employees. Listening to employees' needs and concerns opens the door for improvements and makes building a team that trusts and respects the leadership of the company possible.

If those in leadership positions listen in a defensive manner, always prepared to defend the status quo instead of considering possible changes for the better, eventually subordinates quit trying to communicate at all. They feel defeated before they begin and work at developing an "I don't care" attitude. That attitude spells failure for everyone involved in such one-sided exchanges.

There are few things more motivating than knowing that you have been heard, that your ideas have been considered and that you are taken seriously when you speak your mind. Respect is paramount in all relationships and the quickest way to discount, or show disrespect for, others is to disregard what they have to say. When you know how to listen effectively, you will know how to communicate and motivate effectively as well.

Listen to what Fred Smith says about listening, communicating and understanding. Apply his insights to your daily dealings and you will be amazed at the astounding transformation that takes place in the people you want to motivate to new levels of performance.

Three Questions to Think About

1. How do I know I am being heard?
2. Would others say that I hear them?
3. What will help me be a complete listener?

One Line to Remember

Listen to hear. Speak to be understood.

Scripture to Hide in Your Heart

But your eyes are blessed because they see, and your ears because they hear (Matthew 13:16).

4

LEAVING A LEGACY

Fred's Observation

Lately I have been giving a great deal of thought to the difference between legacy and inheritance. It seems many of my friends are thinking about how to leave money to their families. Although this is admirable, I prefer to think about leaving a legacy. Legacy encompasses how to live and how to die, the passing on of one's core values. My legacy will be my personal answer to the question, "What has been the theme of my life?"

While speaking in Las Vegas years ago, I caught entertainer Ray Bolger's act to get a sense of who he was before I introduced him at the next day's conference. (The limber-bodied Bolger is best known for his portrayal of the Scarecrow in the classic *The Wizard of Oz*.) In his show he performed the signature steps of many great dancers who preceded him, including Bill "Bojangles" Robinson and Fred Astaire. His message was that they left something on the floor when they no longed danced. The closing of his show was a solo spotlight focused on a stool center stage. On it sat Ray Bolger's dance shoes, making the tacit statement that he, too, wanted to "leave something on the floor."

We must carefully consider what legacy we are leaving. I am convinced that inheritances oftentimes split families but that legacies always bond them. How many situations do you know in which second generations argue and even sue over money? The passing of the torch should not ignite a family fire.

It is crucial to think about the imprints that we leave. The "footprints on the sands of time" that the poet writes about speak of the marks we make, the rent we pay for our space on the earth. Our legacy will live on as long as our influence survives. It is our responsibility to make it a good one.

Reflection: Ken Blanchard

CEO, The Blanchard Companies

I think Fred's distinction between legacy and inheritance is important. When our kids were teenagers, my wife, Margie, and I made it clear to them that when we died we weren't going to leave them any money. We didn't know anybody who had truly benefited from being left a bundle of money. Instead, we wanted to pay for opportunities. We paid for their college education, both undergraduate and graduate; we paid for learning opportunities. We paid for family trips. In other words, we used money to create opportunities and family interactions.

We are contributing to a fund now that will pay for the education of our grandchildren. We don't want their parents to worry about that expense.

Jesus talked more about money than He did about anything else in the Bible. He wasn't against making money, but He knew the worship of money was the root of all evil. Therefore, we want any money that we leave to do good and to benefit people, but not give them an opportunity to create something negative in their lives.

Leaving a legacy is much more important to me than leaving an inheritance. I think the legacy you leave is the legacy you live. I am keenly aware that my children and now my grandchildren are watching me. What I want them to look at is my behavior, which will impact their lives and last far beyond my existence.

People ask me all the time, "Who had the biggest impact on your life?" I quickly mention my father and mother. Their impact had nothing to do with the money they made or left (which was negligible) but how they lived their lives. One of the biggest thrills for me is to hear my son and daughter today telling their kids and friends the same things I told them early in life. It warms my heart to realize that maybe some of my musings were valuable to them.

People are watching you. How you live and how you act is your legacy. That is so much more important than your inheritance.

Three Questions to Think About

1. How do I define the difference between legacy and inheritance?
2. What legacy am I building for my business, church, family?
3. What "rent" am I paying for my space on Earth?

One Line to Remember

Our legacy will live on as long as our influence survives.

Scripture to Hide in Your Heart

I have competed well; I have finished the race; I have kept the faith! (2 Timothy 4:7).

5

THE GLORY OF GRACE

Fred's Observation

Grace was genuine, real, personal and palpable to the great saints. Brother Lawrence, Frank Laubach, François Fénelon—these Christian mystics never doubted they were the constant recipients of God's amazing grace. Grace was a practical part of their everyday lives.

For example, Brother Lawrence said that when he made a mistake, he didn't spend any time thinking about it—he just confessed it and moved on. Before I read that, I had been trapped by guilt—immediate grace was too good to be true. Brother Lawrence's experience greatly released me.

Nevertheless, legalism appeals to our common sense and reasoning. I find it necessary to remind myself that the very Scripture that makes me know my guilt lets me know God's grace. By refusing grace, we play God and discipline ourselves. We view events as punishment. We see correction coming, when in reality, it isn't correction at all—it is just a consequence. But we try to read into our circumstances a sense of God's judgment.

Why? Because we feel we deserve judgment rather than grace. Grace brings freedom. If only we could accept grace fully, then we, like Brother Lawrence, could have the freedom to admit failure and move on. Since grace cannot be deserved, why should I feel others are more worthy of it than I am? Or why should I feel they are less worthy? Thinking we can be mature in Christ apart from grace is nothing more than fooling ourselves.

The Bible tells me we should not think too highly of ourselves, but it doesn't advocate "worm thinking" either. We are objects of grace, and grace is a faith gift coming from and through the Father of light.

Reflection: Steve Brown

President, Key Life Network

Author and Professor, Reformed Theological Seminary, Orlando, Florida

My pastor, Pete Alwinson, has a great definition of grace. "Grace," he says, "is doing good for someone when there is no compelling reason to do so and every reason not to."

That's it.

That's what God has done and continues to do for us and, as Fred points out, for the great saints of the Church. Grace is the "good news" that we offer to the world, and it is the good news that we should apply to ourselves . . . but don't.

Yes, there is an appeal to legalism. It is the appeal of common sense, but it is also the appeal of self righteousness and the appeal of earning our way with God so that He owes us. It is a violation of everything the New Testament teaches, and I believe that it, even more than our sin (that's covered), is the consummate sign of our fallen nature.

"Please, Father, I'd rather do it myself."

Then God, as any good father would do, does precisely that. He lets us do it ourselves, and when we have failed miserably and sinned deeply, then we start to understand that, without grace, we don't have a prayer.

Paul said, "Where sin increased, grace abounded all the more" (Romans 5:20, *NASB*). And in that sense, the best gift that we can have in our lives is our sin . . . *when we know it.* And not only that, the most dangerous thing in our lives is our obedience . . . *when we know it.*

My late friend Jack Miller was right when he said that all the Bible can be summed up in two statements: (1) Cheer up, you're a lot worse than you think you are; and (2) cheer up, God's grace is a lot bigger than you think it is.

Three Questions to Think About

1. In what area of my life am I replacing grace with legalism?
2. Why do I struggle with freedom in Christ?
3. What one thing can I do to let grace abound?

One Line to Remember

Thinking that we can be mature in Christ apart from grace is nothing more than fooling ourselves.

Scripture to Hide in Your Heart

I do not set aside God's grace, because if righteousness could come through the law, then Christ died for nothing! (Galatians 2:21).

6

THE VALUE OF HEROES

Fred's Observation

Thomas Carlyle said, "Society is founded on hero worship." History is the story of the impact of great men and women. They shaped their times for good.

But occasionally we need to stop saying great things about our heroes and ask what they would say about us. They can become the verbs in our lives.

Heroes must survive for a long time as examples of trustworthy values, in season and out. It is not just being a winner today that creates a hero. The apostle Paul deserves hero status. Conversely, I know of very few men who emulate Nero. Today we name our children Paul and our dogs Nero.

We should know how to make ourselves small by comparison to our heroes. By humbling ourselves in this positive, healthy way, we see ourselves in light of the values we inherit from our heroes and are able to honestly assess whether we're progressing in virtue. It is this discipline that always inspires and makes room for growth.

In "A Psalm of Life," Henry Wadsworth Longfellow wrote, "Lives of great men all remind us we can make our lives sublime and, departing, leave behind us footprints on the sands of time." Our daughter, Brenda, knew how I enjoyed these lines. On my study wall is a framed board covered with sand and three small footprints—those of her children, then ages one, three and four. In her quiet, persuasive way, she was reminding me that my grandchildren's footsteps are walking somewhat behind my own.

In 2004, my death was momentarily anticipated. In my hospital bed I prayed for my children, grandchildren and great-grandchildren, hoping they would see in me a man of faith. In 2006, I still pray to be a faithful model. Heroes don't have to be famous—they only have to be heroic.

Whose footsteps are you following?

Reflection: Philip Yancey

Best-selling Author and Journalist

As a journalist, I've had the opportunity to choose people I want to emulate, and then go after them for interviews! In other words, I get to track down my heroes, then introduce them to other people.

I've written 20 books, and people often ask me which of these is my favorite. Immediately, I reply, *Soul Survivor*. In that book, I spent a year reflecting on the people who have most influenced me. Some are long dead, people I've known only through their writings (Tolstoy, Dostoevsky, John Donne); and some are active, living people I've come to know through personal interviews (Dr. Paul Brand, Frederick Buechner, Robert Coles, Annie Dillard).

As I think about them as a group, I realize that humility is the one characteristic most of them have in common. These are towering men and women who have changed the world around them, yet they have done so in the spirit of Jesus, by serving others rather than dominating them.

Fred Rogers, host of the children's television show *Mister Rogers' Neighborhood*, used to do a ritual every time he spoke before a crowd. He would ask the audience to pause for a minute of silence and think about all those who had helped them become who they are. Once, in a prestigious gathering at the White House, he was given only eight minutes to address children's issues, and still he devoted one of those minutes to silence. "Invariably, that's what people will remember," he said, "that silence."

I spent a year on my book project. Of course, not everyone has a year to spend sitting around thinking about how other people have affected him or her. It's a wonderful exercise, though, even if you only have five minutes. We become the people we are, not through isolation, but in community with others. Heroes are the people who lead us in the right direction.

Three Questions to Think About

1. What are the common characteristics of my heroes?
2. In what way have I been heroic?
3. What mark am I making in the sands of time?

One Line to Remember

Heroes don't have to be famous—they just have to be heroic.

Scripture to Hide in Your Heart

Be imitators of me, just as I also am of Christ (1 Corinthians 11:1).

7

WORDS TO LIVE BY

Fred's Observation

"Lord, grant us in our work, satisfaction; in our leisure, pleasure; in our study, wisdom; and in our love, loyalty." Years ago while reading, I discovered William Barclay's prayer. I was so impressed with the balance of life he described that I easily memorized it. Through the years I have repeated it to myself many times and twice I have taught it as a Sunday School lesson. The first time I only taught the four requests. Later, I realized that I had missed the significance of the three opening words.

"Lord"—One of the major theological questions today is whether Christ can be Savior without being Lord. George Gallup did a survey among the "born again" and found that only 10 percent considered their faith in daily decision-making. He wrote a book entitled *The Saints Among Us*, indicating that 90 percent of us are nominal Christians.[1]

"Grant"—This reminds us that all good and perfect gifts come from above. We have no demands on God, only requests. Again, the Bible tells us that we have nothing but what we have received of God (see 1 Corinthians 4:7).

"Us"—This reminds us that Christianity is a community, a Body, a family. It is not just an individual experience. It is not like the pine tree that can grow by itself. It is like the redwood that grows in a cluster of trees, with all of the roots supporting the others. Gert Behanna was born and raised in the old Waldorf Astoria amid amazing wealth. After spending much of her life wedded to a lifestyle of drugs and alcohol, she became a Christian. When she prayed "Our Father" she realized that she was a member of a family and gave most of her wealth to needy Christians whom she considered brothers and sisters.

"Lord, grant us," a triad of infinite significance.

Reflection: Howard E. Butt, Jr.

Business Executive

Founder, Laity Lodge and the Howard E. Butt Foundation

Most translations of the Bible never use the word "saint." It's hard to believe, but the New Testament doesn't talk about one saint at a time. We are always God's *saints*—plural. I need others to help me be a saint. I'll never make it alone.

God wants each individual to be more like Christ so that the entire Church will be more like Christ. But none of us can be more like Christ without support from other Christians. I will never be more Christlike without others to help me. That is why Christian life is lived in community.

Even our God is a community. We worship three Persons in One—Father, Son and Holy Spirit. I don't fully understand the Trinity, but I know it indicates community within our one God. Perfect fellowship, perfect harmony, perfect love exists within God Himself.

In our work at Laity Lodge over the past 40 years, we have become more and more convinced about the importance of relationships and community.

Whenever two people get together, one will lead and one will follow, even if they split up, take turns or make war.

Community runs on two legs: equality and leadership. No organization works without a leader—no marriage, no home, no school, no business, no government.

God does not give Himself to us in parts. The whole Trinity lives in us and teaches us to practice both authority and submission.

When we submit, we are servants. When we exert authority, we are leaders. The Holy Spirit teaches us to live in a kind of holy flexibility. We know when to be submissive to other people, and we know how to assert our leadership in the flexible rhythm of everyday life.

Three Questions to Think About

1. Do I live as a pine tree, or a redwood?
2. What am I doing to create community?
3. When do I lead, and when do I follow?

One Line to Remember

Christianity is a community, a Body, a family. It is not just an individual experience.

Scripture to Hide in Your Heart

Let the peace of Christ be in control in your heart (for you were in fact called as one body to this peace), and be thankful (Colossians 3:15).

Note

1. George H. Gallup, *The Saints Among Us* (New York: Morehouse Group, 1992).

8

MEANINGFUL ROUTINES, NOT MUNDANE RUTS

Fred's Observation

I recently had an interesting discussion about ritual versus reality, recognizing that ritual was originally established to perpetuate reality. However, we humans have a tendency to keep the ritual and let the reality slip away. Theologically, this may be a subtle attempt on our part to put ourselves in control of what is actually divine.

When we do this, we feel free to augment the ritual to please ourselves. This way we can make the ritual so elaborate that it becomes what we would want it to be if we were God . . . not bearing much resemblance to the sandals and seamless robe exemplified by Jesus.

Often I have asked husbands if they still kiss their wives as they leave for work. Almost indignantly they will say they do. I have asked them if they have considered the difference between the first kiss on the honeymoon and the one they give now. The first one was probably a pretty mushy one—even a double dip! The husband might have even thought about calling in sick! Now his wife gets a little peck as he hurries through the door on the way to the car. Occasionally they may even miss, but at least they tried—and the ritual goes on, while the reality suffers.

Then we ask, Should vacant ritual be discarded? Not at all. We need, instead, to return the reality to the ritual.

When I was chairman of the Youth for Christ board, I asked a young man why they were trying to destroy the traditions of the Church with contemporary music and casual dress. He replied, "Mr. Smith, we are not trying to destroy the traditions of the faith, but we're not willing to perpetuate them without the experience that created them."

Excellent answer, well said! Uncover the ritual to discover the reality.

Reflection: T. George Harris

Founding Editor, Psychology Today, American Health *and* Spirituality & Health
Contributor, Beliefnet.com

As a teenage forward observer in World War II, I fell into a habit of repeating a buck-passing prayer: "Not my will, but Thine." My main job, from Omaha Beach to Bastogne and on to Ohrdruf concentration camp, was to direct heavy artillery fire at German infantry tanks, and even trains, from a little Piper Cub. We worked as close as we could get to the enemy, usually 4,000 feet or more, but on some foggy days we were down near the treetops. In 116 missions flown under fire over enemy lines or behind them, we had to patch frequent bullet holes in our canvas grasshoppers. Actually, we laughed quite a lot at the misses—after they'd missed.

That same repetitive prayer brought a touch of nonchalance that supported me through most of the major race riots I covered during the school integration struggles and over the years of productive social protest by people reaching deeper for understanding beyond the shallows of pop journalism.

To my surprise, I came to realize that ritual serves a religious purpose, very different from the one I thought I understood. Yes, it helps us rediscover reality in the light of the present, the kind of passionate rediscovery that T. S. Eliot evoked in his Four Quartets, the kind Fred's Youth for Christ friend had in mind when defending guitar music in church.

Beginning with the work of Harvard cardiologist Herbert Benson, it became clear that the body responds in a unique way to the most routine ritual of most faith traditions—a repetitive prayer. I can never be sure what my soul is doing, but it's my body that reports when the Holy Spirit opens a circuit and establishes connectivity. It's the same kind of religious high I get from belting out the familiar, old gut-buster hymns, "Amazing Grace" or "Rock of Ages" and sometimes "Beulah Land."

Three Questions to Think About

1. In what area of my life am I substituting ritual for reality?
2. What is my soul doing?
3. How do I keep challenging the value of tradition?

One Line to Remember

We humans have a tendency to keep the ritual and let the reality slip away.

Scripture to Hide in Your Heart

Thus you nullify the word of God by your tradition that you have handed down. And you do many things like this (Mark 7:13).

9

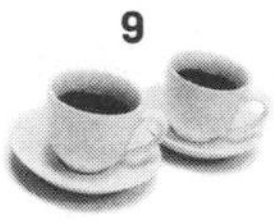

DIVINE PRINCIPLES

Fred's Observation

While Proverbs says, "The fear of the Lord is the beginning of wisdom" (Proverbs 1:7), it does not give us a clear and succinct definition of "wisdom." Personally, I define it as *the knowledge and use of divine principles.* As Einstein said, "I want to think God's thoughts after Him." To me, that is wisdom. Too many people move from data to information to knowledge but never get to wisdom.

The wisdom of divine principles is often conceptual, not in chapter and verse. For example, the love of God that so few people really understand was perfectly stated by Ray Stedman in these words: "My life changed when I realized God was for me."

The gaining of knowledge is the first step toward wisdom. For example, my good friend Jack Modesett, Jr., said, "My time at Princeton became enjoyable and profitable when I discovered that learning was fun." He has carried this over into his Bible studies and teaching. Exploring divine mysteries is exciting.

Another helpful divine principle is "God will not do for you what you can do for yourself, but He will not let you do for yourself what only He can do." Often we must take the first step, like the priests who had to step into the Red Sea before the waters parted.

A principle that has been very sustaining to me in my disability is one that Oswald Chambers has helped me see:

"God will not give you strength to overcome, but will give you strength *as* you overcome." What a treasury of wisdom we have in the saints who have gone before us, and when we accept Scripture as God's Word and the authority for life.

The fear of the Lord is the beginning of wisdom and obedience is the end.

Reflection: Jack Modesett, Jr.

Houston Businessman and Recipient of the Christianity Today International Fred Smith Leadership Award

A number of years ago I sent Fred Smith an article from the *Wall Street Journal* on business practices in Japan, asking him if he could find any principles that might be helpful. He sent the article back covered with marginal notes, and listing dozens of things I had not seen!

Intrigued, I began to look for principles as I studied and taught the Bible.

At first, it was hard to dig them out. But as I continued to look, more became apparent, and I got better at expressing them in ways that I could remember. In the parable of the wise and foolish virgins, I found two that I've never forgotten: "God honors preparation" and "There is safety in surplus." These two are universal, whether you are talking about business or preparing a Sunday School lesson.

I then began to notice that other good communicators used the same technique. Ray Stedman said that "truth acted upon" is one of the most important principles by which God governs the universe. Another from Ray is "The flesh cannot be fixed: It must be killed."

Chuck Swindoll saw that the life of David teaches that "it is devotion, not perfection, that warms the heart of God."

Oswald Chambers is a great source of principles such as "Beware of posing as a profound person. God became a baby." And again, "God does not forgive because He loves you. He forgives you because Christ died for you."

Fénelon is a goldmine of principles such as "Self-love is touchy, and when wounded screams murderer!"

Looking for principles is fun and rewarding. And with a little practice, it becomes a way of seeing God at work in His creation. Thanks, Fred, for launching me on that road.

Three Questions to Think About

1. What biblical truth is changing my life?
2. How am I learning to "dig out" God's principles?
3. What concepts am I teaching others?

One Line to Remember

The wisdom of divine principles is often conceptual, not in chapter and verse.

Scripture to Hide in Your Heart

To obey the Lord is the fundamental principle for wise living; all who carry out his precepts acquire good moral insight. He will receive praise forever (Psalm 111:10).

10

THE ART OF CRITICISM

Fred's Observation

Keep criticism positive. Recently, I tried to analyze the reasons I criticize—and I think they are probably the reasons all of us have a tendency to criticize. Three reasons were negative and one was positive.

The number one reason that we criticize is that we are just passing the buck on a self-grudge. If before 10:00 in the morning I have been critical of everybody and everything, I must stop and ask, "Fred, what is wrong with you? What are you mad at yourself about?" And generally, I have to go and make a call to somebody and apologize. My environment won't straighten out until I quit being mad at myself and make it right.

The second reason: We criticize to show superior knowledge. How often does some fellow show you a great idea and you respond enthusiastically until you suddenly say to yourself, *I can't be too enthusiastic because he may feel he is as smart as I am*. So you say, "Joe, this is a great idea, but . . ." Many "yes, buts" come from the desire to show your superior knowledge.

The third reason for negative criticism is usually performance that hasn't made the grade. Those who start well but don't make the "A-list" usually become critics. You can't put a failed executive back into the ranks—he will become a naysayer.

Positive criticism, on the other hand, is simply a desire to bring improvement—to *help* someone else by pointing out something he or she might not see. It is done quietly and kindly. True positive criticism is not done within the earshot of others (unlike the three negative types, which are shouted gleefully before an audience!). True, strong, positive criticism is specific and directed clearly toward the area that needs work for the sake of improvement. The motive of positive criticism—helping the other person—sets it apart from the negative forms.

When you criticize positively, you are demonstrating emotional stability—a quality every leader must have.

Reflection: Ron Glosser

President and CEO (Retired), Hershey Trust Company

Fred and I have spent enough time together that he knows that I want to spend most of my time being an encourager. When I find myself being overly critical, it is time for self-examination. I believe that criticism should be used sparingly. It is good to ask myself the question, *Is this something the individual would like to improve if he or she knew that it would be helpful?*

Our good mutual friend Ken Blanchard has made a strong case for "one minute praises." In my experience, I have found this very true and most constructive. There are times when criticism is needed, but in most situations praising will produce far better results over time.

During the years I was CEO of Hershey Trust Company, I made it a rule to evaluate those who reported to me on a quarterly basis. I found this eliminated major surprises at year's end when evaluating for compensation and promotion. It is hard to fault an individual who believes he or she is doing well when we haven't taken the time to discuss areas of needed improvement. If after discussing these areas of needed improvement and not seeing change, it is fair to have a serious discussion as to whether or not the individual should be retained as part of the team.

I have found that the best way to keep from being overly critical is to get myself centered early in the day. For me, this is achieved by reading the Scriptures and praying. I try to identify myself as the beloved child of God and to see all those with whom I come in contact that same way.

Three Questions to Think About

1. How do I react to constructive criticism?
2. What mood is my best for receiving helpful counsel?
3. What form of criticism is my *modus operandi* at home, at work, at church?

One Line to Remember

When you criticize positively you are demonstrating emotional stability—a quality every leader must have.

Scripture to Hide in Your Heart

Besides, we have experienced discipline from our earthly fathers and we respected them; shall we not submit ourselves all the more to the Father of spirits and receive life? (Hebrews 12:9).

11

LIVING THROUGH LOVE

Fred's Observation

Love creates an environment that strengthens the will to live. Love brings joy to our life when there is little to rejoice about. We appreciate being loved so much that we sometimes forget the responsibility that comes with being loved: Those who love us want us to live, not die. We often talk about pursuing a life worth living, and I am convinced that understanding the value of love is a tremendous part of that endeavor. Many tell me that I am too strong-willed to die, but I believe that the realization that I can contribute and I am loved gives me purpose.

Doctors say that many old people who are said to die of natural causes really die of loneliness. Current medical research shows that we can literally die of broken hearts. Conversely, studies show that people who receive care and prayer tend to live longer and richer lives than those who don't.

Just as God's greatest gift to us is His love, so our greatest gift to one another should be our love for others—and for Him. Love does not need to be earned; it is given. And so, no matter how incapacitated we are, we can still experience being loved—and loving.

Love is the strongest sustaining emotion we can feel. Acts of love are as important as words of love. One of my favorite times in the day is when my daughter, Brenda, comes in, pats me on the arm, kisses me on the forehead and says, "I will see you in the morning." When I was pronounced "dying" by my doctor, she said, "No, I will take him home and he will live." That is exactly what happened. There is power in love.

Even though my bride of 67 years is now in heaven, I still celebrate Valentine's Day—for her. Now, every day is filled with God's love.

Reflection: Ruth Stafford Peale

Chairman Emeritus of Guideposts, Incorporated
Author and Speaker

Fred speaks of the "responsibility of love." One of the secrets to the love that my husband, Norman Vincent Peale, and I shared is that we were both interested in the same things and thought along the same lines in so many situations. We both worked hard at helping people, and I think that is why we were married for more than 60 years. Although we were both always very busy, we recognized that our visions were the same.

We also recognized the unique gifts God had given each of us. In fact, soon after we were married, I discovered that in one respect my husband and I were exactly the opposite. I never had any problem making up my mind about much of anything, but Norman often struggled with decisions. Often he asked for my advice, and I would stop what I was doing and try to listen patiently. Most of the time he just needed me as a sounding board to help clarify his thinking.

Many times, to my astonishment, I found the next day that the matter was not settled at all, that he wanted to review it again, that maybe there were angles we had not considered seriously enough. Part of love, for me, was learning to be his ear and to help him talk through his decisions.

I concluded that if God was going to guide our lives, I was going to have to keep my mind open so that Norman and I could use the gifts we had each been given. We were a partnership, each using and developing our own gifts while moving together in the same direction.

I often wondered, *Do I have to make these adjustments forever?* The answer was a resounding yes, because we never stop growing—even after 63 years of marriage. I came to the realization that only a woman can be a wife, and only a wife can give unique help to her husband. No truth was ever as difficult for me to embrace as this, but the rewards were—and always will be—tremendous.

Three Questions to Think About

1. Whom do I love, and who loves me?
2. What are the responsibilities that come with being loved?
3. How do I recognize God's love in my life?

One Line to Remember

Love creates an environment that strengthens the will to live.

Scripture to Hide in Your Heart

And now these three remain: faith, hope, and love. But the greatest of these is love (1 Corinthians 13:13).

12

ENERGIZED BY ACCOMPLISHMENT

Fred's Observation

I have learned that if I end my day feeling beat, I probably didn't accomplish much that is worthwhile. Accomplishment gives me such joy that it actually restores my energy. Activity for its own sake, on the other hand, is draining.

As I have gotten older, I have found I am more selective, more thorough, more conscious of what I am trying to do. I have learned that activity is not the mark of accomplishment. The more I can delegate tasks that are not uniquely mine, the more attention I can pay to those that are. Do you ever catch yourself doing someone else's work? Why? My friend who was head of a large international company once told me, "I am not going to pay them and do their work, too."

A leader may feel that he or she doesn't have the luxury of only doing a few things well, but the principles still apply. I have run small organizations, and I have run large corporations. I have never been short of time, because I believe I know how to prioritize. I keep for myself the things that only I can do and delegate the rest. But many fall prey to the temptation to keep others dependent upon them in order to make themselves feel important.

I don't get joy from feeling needed. I have told my family that when I die, I want them to remember our love, not an unhealthy dependence. I want them each to mature to the point where they don't need me. I never want to be like the criminal who, seeing himself on the post office wall, quipped, "It is so good to be wanted!"

To me, doing what only I can do is a proper leadership philosophy. Many leaders tie their ego to activity and forget that results are the measure, not the fact that they turn out the lights at night.

Reflection: Garry D. Kinder

Founder and Co-President, The Kinder Group, Inc.
Author, Speaker and Teacher, Prestonwood Bible Study
Founder, Roaring Lambs

Never confuse activity with accomplishment. A person walking in circles is exerting the same amount of energy as someone walking down the street. But one is going somewhere, while the other is not. We do not want activity; we want results. We are not paid for activity; we are paid for results.

Fred is also saying we need to discipline ourselves to do what we ought to do. We need to delegate what we shouldn't do. Always do what you do best. Stick with your passion.

In college I had a very fine professor my senior year. His name was Dr. William T. Beetles. I remember him using this illustration to teach us a very important lesson: If you had an attorney who was the best attorney in town, but who also happened to be the best typist in town, who should do the typing in his law firm, him or his secretary? The answer is obvious.

In our businesses we need to work at the right priorities. We need to spend our time on the high-pay-off activities.

Many people work at things they enjoy and do well but that don't pay big dividends. Work at projects that energize you. Stay away from anything that leaves you feeling drained at the end of the day.

We should always be building on our strengths and managing around our weaknesses. Peter Drucker has always taught us to build on strengths and our weaknesses will become irrelevant. If we work on our weaknesses, then our strengths will become irrelevant.

Three Questions to Think About

1. How do I focus on accomplishment and not just activity?
2. What work should I be delegating to others?
3. What are my key strengths?

One Line to Remember

I don't get joy from feeling needed. I have told my family that when I die, I want them to remember our love, not an unhealthy dependence.

Scripture to Hide in Your Heart

Moses' father-in-law said to him, "What you are doing is not good! You will surely wear out, both you and these people who are with you, for this is too heavy a burden for you; you are not able to do it by yourself" (Exodus 18:17-18).

13

AVOIDING A BITTER TASTE

Fred's Observation

The little black book that some use as a "get-even-with list" is a poison package. The Scriptures tell us, "Vengeance is mine, I will repay" (Hebrews 10:30, *NASB*). Vengeance has no place in the mature life—it is acid that eats away at the inner being.

Some individuals have been unfortunate enough to build their life around one incident of hurt, working at revenge until it becomes the obsession of a lifetime. It makes them mean-spirited, cynical, unhealthy, desperate, joyless and certainly unpleasant to be around.

It's difficult for any of us to avoid becoming bitter when we have been hurt. Sometimes our hurt is caused by an individual, sometimes by a particular situation. We all know men and women who are living with the fallout from abusive experiences, physical ailments or irreparable emotional damage. We know those who handle hurt with grace and others who face each day with a chip on their shoulder.

After speaking to a prayer breakfast in Wichita, Kansas, I was asked by one of the executives present to go out and see a plant that employed 200 mentally handicapped people. He was chairman of the board of the company, and he was insistent that we make this visit. I must admit that this plant wasn't number one on my list of stops to make while I was in town, but I'm glad he persisted.

Most of the employees at the plant had Down syndrome. As we toured the plant, I asked him how often he came out, and he said, "Almost every day." I could tell he was very much loved because employees were constantly coming up to greet and hug him. When we got to the gymnasium, a Down syndrome child came up and enthusiastically embraced him. He turned to me and said, "Fred, this is our daughter, Lynn." I hugged her, too, and realized that instead of being bitter, he had become better.

Reflection: Verdell Davis Kreisher
Author, Speaker and Grief Counselor

Sometimes life just hurts, and we don't understand why it has to be so. More than that, we scream out in our pain: "It's not fair!" The cry for fairness comes from the sense that someone in particular or life in general owes us something. Our Western culture breeds a sense of entitlement in each of us. How often do we find ourselves saying things such as "I ought to have," "I deserve," "Why me?" "Where's my fair share?" "Why can't I?" So when life hands me lemons, I am faced with one very big choice. As Fred put it, *Am I going to become better or bitter?*

The living of life will eventually bring each of us face to face with some measure of the realities of life in a broken world: Not every illness is cured, not every relationship is mended, not every airplane comes home. Somewhere in time we each will find ourselves standing in the rubble of what was, wondering, *What now?* Lifestorms I call them—the "not supposed to bes" of life: death, violated relationships, betrayal, children born with disabilities and deformities, disease, man's inhumanity to man, moral failures, tragedies, vulnerability to terrorism . . . and yet . . .

And yet. Those words are pregnant with possibility. It was an airplane that didn't come home that taught me that my brokenness in my own hands remains brokenness and gathers to itself anger, bitterness, rage, cynicism, desperation and emotional bondage. And yet that same brokenness in the hands of the One who alone has the power to bring new life out of the ashes of the old will become so much more. He will indeed bend down with us as we pick up the shattered pieces of life as we once knew it. And in the bending will infuse us with strength and grace that can show to a cynical world that even the darkest of tragedies can become a pillar of light.

The choice is ours.

Three Questions to Think About

1. How is a personal hurt defining me?
2. In what ways am I choosing to be better, not bitter?
3. How am I dealing with my "not supposed to bes"?

One Line to Remember

The most successful people I know have decided to become better, not bitter.

Scripture to Hide in Your Heart

But I trust in you, O LORD! I declare, "You are my God!" (Psalm 31:14).

14

CREATING A WINNING ENVIRONMENT

Fred's Observation

When I saw the old wrangler on whose life the movie *The Horse Whisperer* was based, I felt that he was a kindred spirit. He used empathy rather than dominance to achieve his goals. He transformed both the role of the wrangler and the experience of the horse by moving from a hierarchical system, which was tyrannical, to a team, or mutual-interest, program. He no longer depended on the horse's fear but on its friendship. His orders became friendly suggestions that he knew would be accepted.

The famed "winningest coach," John Wooden of UCLA basketball, used his own nondictatorial system. Reportedly, he never mentioned the word "win" to any of his teams. He simply emphasized the concept of doing one's best. This was an entirely different emphasis from the usual pre-game chatter in the locker rooms of his day. Wooden's philosophy excluded using dirty tricks, bending the rules, violating recruiting regulations and falsifying grades, all of which winning teams often rationalize. Wooden made it possible to win even when losing (which wasn't often), as long as the men on his teams did their best. He had an eye for talent and for men who would grow in an atmosphere that demanded their best. He built teams of honorable men.

We lead to accomplish the vision of our calling. We optimize our associates' gifts and passions as we work to attain what we genuinely believe is the will of God, for the glory of God.

We work to find the uniqueness in others and then to develop, encourage and reward it. We work to find our own reward, desiring to hear one day: "Well done, good and faithful servant" (Matthew 25:23, *NIV*).

Catching a vision and then creating an atmosphere in which talented men and women thrive is the role of the leader. Working together in tandem, not working for a tyrant, is the sign of a healthy organization.

Reflection: Bill Glass

CEO Emeritus, Champions for Life
Former All-Pro, Cleveland Browns
All-American, Baylor University

My earliest memories were of a father who sat on my bedside each night before I slept. He told me what a fine boy I was and how I was going to accomplish great things. It was a great blessing to have a father who was so positive—but too soon it was bewildering to be without him, for he died when I was only 14. I longed for his hugs and for his manly strength and stability.

But then I met a coach, Bill Stages. He'd been raised in the Masonic home in Fort Worth without mother or dad. He must have heard that I was now fatherless. All I know is that every day after football practice he stayed out with me to practice defensive line plays. Often after workout he'd walk beside me with his hand on my shoulder or with his arm around me. He was always positive, assuring me I was getting better each day. I was easily the slowest, smallest, most frightened player on the team. I often thought, *How could I possibly be the younger brother of the greatest player in Corpus Christi football history?* Heck, I didn't even like football.

But I kept trying because my coach would loudly proclaim my successes and ignore my failures. I soon became unblockable. It didn't hurt that I had constant drilling and weightlifting and that I gained 60 pounds and 6 inches in 1 year. But the main thing was that I was getting the feel of a dad who sat on my bed at night and blessed me. It's amazing what we can accomplish by receiving a blessing.

The greatest blessing is that of our heavenly Father, but often it is received best when shown by our earthly fathers. Thanks, Fred, for being a surrogate father to me.

Three Questions to Think About

1. What blessing have I received in my life?
2. How have I responded to the lack of a particular blessing?
3. How can I bless my family and friends?

One Line to Remember

We lead to accomplish the vision of our calling.

Scripture to Hide in Your Heart

I no longer call you slaves, because the slave does not understand what his master is doing. But I have called you friends, because I have revealed to you everything I heard from my Father (John 15:15).

15

DOING MY BEST

Fred's Observation

As Christians, we need to remember that God is interested in our work—He commands us to be excellent, "not slothful," in business. I am sure that He is hurt when we slip into mediocrity, standing around the water cooler complaining or sneaking into the restroom to use our cell phones. When we use our business computers on company time for personal business or entertainment, we dishonor Him. He says to us, "Whatsoever your hand finds to do, do it with all of your might, as unto the Lord" (see Colossians 3:23). Notice, it doesn't say, "If you enjoy your work, like the boss or even enjoy your associates." It says that if we are going to put our life into it, we should do it to the best of our ability. "Unto the Lord" gives work a divine significance.

Christian executive Mason Roberts, former president of Frigidaire, shared with me his daily closing ritual. He had a daily calendar with the words "Having done my best today, it will be easier to do better tomorrow" printed on the top. At the end of the day, he would go to the calendar, put his hand on the current day's page, give a short prayer of thanksgiving for the day, tear off the page, throw it in the wastebasket and go home. On those rare days when he could not honestly pray that he had done his best, he would call his wife and ask her to delay dinner so that he could feel that satisfaction.

It is our responsibility to bring meaning to our work. We can do it in three ways: (1) in being excellent in what we do, which gives us self-respect and security; (2) in the attitude we take to the job, which helps create a positive environment; and (3) in seeing our associates as those we can encourage and even bring to the Lord.

Reflection: Harold Myra
Author, Chairman and CEO (Retired), Christianity Today International

Excellence. The word has been stamped on leadership literature for decades. What starts our engines to drive toward it? How do those engines constantly refuel and lubricate mile after mile, year after year, decade after decade? How can the quest for excellence result in a lifetime of productivity, service and growth?

We often refer to a "corporate mandate" for a CEO. Without a mandate, the CEO lacks focus and stumbles. The person who wants to burst through inertia and press toward excellence needs a personal mandate, and for me, that starts with a sense of call.

It's a two-way communication. I've often quoted Jeremiah 33:3: "Call to Me and I will answer you, and show you great and mighty things" (*NKJV*). We call on God for guidance, and then hopefully we have that sense of call, not necessarily to a specific vocation but to follow the Spirit, who then energizes the drive toward excellence.

In the mid-1970s, after Fred had engineered my becoming president, CEO and publisher of Christianity Today International (CTI) at age 35, I kept looking to him for wise counsel. One day on the phone, he said, in regard to CTI's board politics, "Well, you know who the boss is, don't you?"

My instant reply was, "Of course. God."

Now Fred was looking for a different answer. He was emphasizing that I had to recognize Billy Graham, CTI's founder, as the one to whom the Trustees would look for final decisions. It may have felt to Fred that I was a bit like the Sunday School kid who answers every question with "Jesus."

Yet my instinctive answer about the Boss rang true in my own soul. I sensed that the volatility at CTI at that time was beyond my control, and that whatever God was going to do would happen. My responsibility was to press for excellence in product, in relationships, in spiritual integrity. If it all came unglued, the ultimate Boss would make the ultimate decisions.

This providential perspective allows us the freedom to press toward excellence while leaving the results in God's hands. It starts with the call, but if our efforts fail, if we crash and burn in our work because of external circumstances, we rise up and get going again.

The Spirit urges us toward excellence. Just as in corporate life, this kind of mandate brings focus critical to sustaining the quest for excellence in all areas of life, with all its jarring reversals as well as its triumphs.

Three Questions to Think About

1. Where do I see excellence in my life?
2. What is my call?
3. How do I apply "as unto the Lord" at work, home, church?

One Line to Remember

"Unto the Lord" gives work a divine significance.

Scripture to Hide in Your Heart

And whatever you do in word or deed, do it all in the name of the Lord Jesus, giving thanks to God the Father through him (Colossians 3:17).

16

READING LIFE'S ROAD SIGNS

Fred's Observation

Choosing a goal in life is not our most important decision—choosing our direction is. Chasing short-range goals can take us in the wrong direction. Mature success and satisfaction come from the direction in which we move, not in the goals that we attain.

Too much goal orientation brings us the same problem that Harvard Business School found in the "case study" system of teaching. Bright young students learned to solve problems rather than identify opportunities. The real progress in life comes in recognizing opportunities. Problem solving is important, but it is just a means of taking advantage of opportunities. When we become too goal-oriented, we become almost mechanical in our approach to life. The totally technological vantage point tends to turn us into computers. Who wants that?

I oppose setting an ultimate goal for one's life, in the sense of a specific, definable, measurable place in life at which one hopes to arrive. This puts too much importance on one decision over another. This deterministic approach creates a sense of futility in those who attain what they have aimed for, what they have defined as success and what they see as the "end all." Too often they realize that it was the attaining, not the attainment, that energized them. The becoming is the joy in the journey.

I am not opposed to planning, but I am much more interested in making decisions based on the impact they will have on who I will ultimately become if I follow the path of that decision. I don't want to be so focused on goals that I get to the top of the ladder only to see that it is leaning against the wrong wall.

Goals are important as mile markers to confirm that we are traveling in the right direction. They are never to be an end in themselves.

Reflection: Margarita C. Treviño
Professor, Dallas Baptist University
Conference Speaker and Writer

I applaud Fred Smith's emphasis on choosing the right direction in life versus being overly engrossed in the achievement of personal goals. Once a goal is identified and launched, it develops a life of its own—an inherent energy that propels forward movement. However laudable, the goal must have wise governance to ultimately create positive change. Proper direction is indispensable.

I want to back up a bit and reflect on a prerequisite to the enunciation of goals and direction in life. I believe we must first *discover our assignment*. It's our *purpose* in life. It is not something we choose. Purpose, in turn, dictates goals and direction.

God told Jeremiah, "Before I formed you in your mother's womb I chose you; before you were born I set you apart; I appointed you to be a prophet to the nations" (Jeremiah 1:5). The same applies to you and me. Before we were born, God deposited an assignment within us. He created us to solve a specific problem.

Dr. Mike Murdock, founder and senior pastor of The Wisdom Center, writes, "You are here on assignment. Everything God created is a solution to a problem." He characterizes one's assignment as follows:

- Your Assignment is always to a person or a people.
- Your Assignment determines the suffering and attacks you will encounter.
- What grieves you is a clue to what you are assigned to heal and restore.
- What grieves you the most reveals the greatest gifts you contain.
- Your Assignment is geographical.
- You will only succeed when your Assignment becomes an obsession.
- Your Assignment requires seasons of preparation.
- Your Assignment may be misunderstood by your own family and those closest to you.
- Your Assignment will always have an enemy. [He adds] Your enemies are as necessary as your friends. Your friends provide comfort. Your enemy provides promotion.
- Your Assignment is the only place your financial provision is guaranteed.[1]

The discovery of our assignment and our submission of that assignment to God's perfect will are the most important steps in the journey we call life.

Three Questions to Think About

1. What is my assignment?
2. In what area of my life have I substituted good goals for a better direction?
3. How do I make sure that my ladder is against the right wall?

One Line to Remember

The becoming is the joy in the journey.

Scripture to Hide in Your Heart

We must . . . run with endurance the race set out for us, keeping our eyes fixed on Jesus, the pioneer and perfecter of our faith (Hebrews 12:1-2).

Note

1. Dr. Mike Murdock, *The Assignment, Volumes 1-2, The Mike Murdock Collector's Edition* (Denton, TX: Wisdom International, 2002).

17

A FAITHFUL FOLLOWER

Fred's Observation

In our lives, "faith" is both a noun and a verb. As a noun we express what is *the* faith. Dr. Ramesh Richard, a famous theologian with two earned PhDs and an international proclaimer of the gospel, gave me the "Five Alones" of the faith: (1) by grace alone, (2) through faith alone, (3) with Scripture alone, (4) in Christ alone, and (5) for God's glory alone. These truths are *the* faith.

Faith, as a verb, is how we live *the* faith out in our lives. By faith we follow the Scriptures both in principles and disciplines for life. We look to the Scriptures for commands and promises.

One time when I was in negotiations with the steelworkers' union, our lawyer was convinced that they were going on strike. Therefore, he recommended that we not make an offer because it would be used as the basis for the next negotiation. As I left home to go to the meeting, I did something I had never done before. I opened the Bible and read the first verse that I saw: "Do not withhold from workers money that is due them" (see James 5:4). I knew what my decision would be. Against the lawyer's recommendation, I opted to make a reasonable offer. To our amazement, the union members readily accepted it. So we avoided a strike. I felt that I had been given divine guidance.

Any time we make a decision to do right, rather than wrong, we are living by faith. Like the old hymn says, to walk in faith a life that pleases God we must trust and obey.

Reflection: Ramesh Richard

Professor, Dallas Theological Seminary
President, Ramesh Richard Evangelism and Church Health [RREACH]

The street definition of "faith" is "to believe what you know isn't true," but the biblical understanding of "faith," a paraphrase of the technical definition of Hebrews 11:1, is "to believe something that you know is true, but can't presently see." In a simple and yet profound distinction, biblical faith can be classified with two prepositions: "through" and "by."

"Through faith" conveys the *instrumental* meaning of faith. Salvation is the gift of God received by grace *through* faith (see Ephesians 2:8-9), and we are not to try to find salvation through any other means. God's eternal salvation is provided through faith alone in the Lord Jesus alone as the only God who saves sinners.

Spiritual vitality is *through* faith. The error of the Galatians that the apostle Paul so forcefully corrected was their quick fall from faith-based to works-based sanctification. The graces of Christian living arrive, to echo Fred Smith, through the pipe of faith, rather than the pump of works. The application is that any spiritual discipline that attempts to manipulate God's favor (e.g., reading the Bible to influence His blessing on a business deal) falls into a works mode of spirituality. God can differentiate between the faithfulness of love and the love of faithfulness. The latter is a faulty spirituality.

"By faith" expresses the *efficient* meaning of faith. When Jesus marvels at "great" faith or chides "little" faith (as in Luke 7:9), He is addressing a quality of faith itself. Christian convictions are *by* faith. That is, we are increasingly convinced of what the Scriptures reveal. Since faith is contrary to *human* wisdom, not to wisdom per se, we grow by faith into convictions that what God says is true. Almost every one of our beliefs ("belief" and "faith" come from the same word in Scripture) is *by* faith. Whether it is believing in the Trinity, the Second Coming of Christ as Judge, or the reality of eternal life, all of these we increasingly grasp by faith.

Christian conduct, especially in ministry, is *by* faith. To decide and live rightly, as Fred notes above, is living by faith. The heroes of Hebrews 11 set out to serve, sacrifice and suffer for God by faith. They were convinced about His purposes, even without circumstantial verification, and continued in God's promises. Are you increasing in your confidence in what God has called and gifted you to do for His glory, His people and His kingdom? Are you obeying Him, when sight says it can't be done?

In the Bible, faith is not contrary to knowledge but is *the opposite of sight*. When we get to heaven, we will not need additional knowledge, for we will have sight. We will be known even as we are known (see 1 John 3:2). Fully! Yet how do we *know* this? By faith.

I am a man of little faith in a great God. Like the desperate father who asked Jesus to heal his son in Mark 9:24, I constantly cry, "I believe; help my unbelief!" Let the nouns become verbs.

Three Questions to Think About

1. In what is my faith rooted?
2. How is my faith lived out at work, in my family, among friends?
3. Do I live by faith in the saving work of Christ on the cross, or do I try to derive grace from "the pump of works"?

One Line to Remember

Any time we make a decision to do right, rather than wrong, we are living by faith.

Scripture to Hide in Your Heart

But someone will say, "You have faith and I have works." Show me your faith without works and I will show you faith by my works (James 2:18).

18

BEING A "CAN DO" LEADER

Fred's Observation

I was interested recently in a survey that studied the difference between successful and unsuccessful businesses. The top executives of major companies were studied. The one outstanding difference between the successful and the unsuccessful executive was that the successful executive says, "I will," while the unsuccessful says, "I should. I ought to. I expect to. I intend to get around to it." (Or as we say in Texas, "I am fixin' to.")

Nothing happens until someone says, "I will." This is the action of the decisive individual. He picks up a great idea. He writes it down, goes back to his office and says, "I will." And he does it. "She" does, too, as my daughter often reminds me! The other guy may get a great idea, may write it down, but then go back to the office and say, "I will get around to this shortly." Shortly seldom comes, so he sits in the same easy chair in the same rut—the one that leads to failure.

The only difference between failure and success is this one point. The successful people say "I will" and they do it. They create a successful plan *and do*. Too many unsuccessful people get ready, aim . . . but fail to fire. The line between success and failure is very thin but very real.

My friends in the insurance industry say it this way: "The successful agent does what the unsuccessful one won't." The successful agent makes the calls, does the prospecting and asks for the signature. The "former" insurance agent organized the forms, read the sales magazines and waited for the right time to make the call. Did it come? Apparently not.

Right thinking followed by right action leads to success.

Reflection: Jack Kinder

Founder and Co-President, Kinder Brothers, International
Author, Speaker and Consultant

The sure way to achieve consistent success is to form the habit of forcing productive activity. The key here is to *form the habit.*

Andrew Carnegie is reported to have rewarded a young consultant, Ivy Lee, with a $25,000 check for bringing to U.S. Steel this simple, habit-building strategy: At the end of each day, all employees were expected to sit down and identify the many things to be done the following day. On a second piece of paper, these tasks were to be listed in the order of their priority.

At the start of each day, the employees were expected to start at the top of their list and scratch out tasks as completed. Moving from top to bottom, they seldom marked out all of their planned activities. However, they did *form the habit* of focusing on the high-priority jobs.

Andrew Carnegie judged the idea to be worth $25,000 to his companies. What will it be worth to you?

Three Questions to Think About

1. What moves me from "I ought" to "I will"?
2. What good habits carry me through the rough times?
3. How do I control my daily activities?

One Line to Remember

Nothing happens until someone says, "I will."

Scripture to Hide in Your Heart

Those who wait for the Lord's help find renewed strength; they rise up as if they had eagles' wings, they run without growing weary, they walk without getting tired (Isaiah 40:31).

19

PREPARED BY HOPE

Fred's Observation

The three important words at the close of 1 Corinthians 13 are "faith," "hope" and "love." Is Paul making a climactic statement that hope is more than faith and love is more than hope? I don't know, but I do know that hope is one of the great controlling emotions in our life. Faith is largely present, hope is largely future, and love is ultimate and everlasting. Hope is our belief in the future based on Christ, who holds it. Hope is not about the seen, but about the unseen.

As the philosopher said, "A man [or woman] can stand almost anything as long as there is hope." When hope goes, desperation and despair soon follow. The Scripture says, "Hope deferred makes the heart sick" (Proverbs 13:12, *NIV*).

I have a Polish physical therapist whose job it is to stretch my muscles back into usefulness after months and months in a bed. I find that when he counts out loud, I have hope of his quitting. When he doesn't count out loud, I miss knowing when the end is. Hope energizes patience. It gives reason for tenacity. It promotes discipline in accomplishment.

The source of hope is not hoping in hope but in hoping specifically in something or someone. We hope in Christ; we hope in our experience or belief that life has a purpose even when we don't see it. Hope requires a definable object. That hope can be eternity—"the blessed hope"—or the assurance that hope gives us here on Earth. My wife's favorite hymn was

"Take the Name of Jesus with You." The chorus has a phrase that describes the nature of Jesus' name: "hope of earth and joy of heaven." Another great hymn line is, "My hope is built on nothing less than Jesus' blood and righteousness."

Hope has substance because we are grounded in a changeless God who is the same as He was in the past, is now in the present and will be in the future.

Reflection: H. Johanna Fisher

Radio Personality and Former Host, Johanna Live!

On leaving a major organization after 10 years of employment, I had tremendous hope that the next step was just a couple of weeks away. It turned out to be more like five months of time in which hope reigned supreme. The move took much longer than anticipated, but during that time I was able to take a solid look at my relationship with the Lord and who I was becoming as a result of it. Hope gave me a place to live as the Lord taught me and worked out the details of the transition. Looking back on it now, it still brings a smile to my face. I had no idea all that was taking place in the heavenlies. But I knew—hoped, believed, understood—that He was doing something for my good.

Hope is not the trivial word that we utter at times: "Oh, I *hope* so." Using it in that way smacks of American colloquialisms that are filled with goose pimply and vague meanings.

Mom often guardedly used the expression "Live in hope; die in despair." Immediately she would add, "That's what they say, but that's not the Christian way to feel." She knew that in Christ there is always hope. Through years of walking with Him, she hoped in His promises.

The Brooklyn Tabernacle Choir sings, "God is working even now." Get it? Believing is seeing clearly.

Who knew that I'd have a chance to revisit that word? This time it's leaving a job after 23 years of doing what I have absolutely enjoyed. The word "hope" is as a mantra to me, because I believe more than ever that God's purpose in my life—and yours!—will be fulfilled at His timing, as we hope and trust in Him. Remind me of that if you happen to see me not reflecting that truth!

Three Questions to Think About

1. In what is my hope grounded?
2. How do I daily remind myself of my hope in a changeless God?
3. What allows me to encourage others to hope?

One Line to Remember

Hope has substance because we are grounded in a changeless God who is the same as He was in the past, is now in the present and will be in the future.

Scripture to Hide in Your Heart

I desperately long for your deliverance. I find hope in your word (Psalm 119:81).

20

KEEPING THE ENGINE IN GEAR

Fred's Observation

During times when we have no great career accomplishments, it is important to have outside achievements. This is the way we re-attach our ego to our accomplishments.

I suggested that a friend who was going through a low time after selling his company find personal satisfaction in a non-career arena. Several months later I saw him, and to my surprise he had lost 40 pounds. He said, "I took your suggestion and it is working—not only have I lost the weight that I badly needed to lose, but I've also won the doubles tennis championship at the club." He had rediscovered the joy of achievement.

Every career has its dead spots. Inevitably there are idling times as we hit plateaus on the climb. It is important to remember that we haven't failed, only our plans have. Rather than letting it throw us off track, we can redirect our productive energies in an avocational direction. We can channel our need for accomplishment into charitable or ministry outlets. We can develop new skills and broaden our current interests. It is important to acknowledge the importance of productivity.

The lull in the career won't kill the proper use of ego gratification. It is important, of course, that these ancillary accomplishments do not become an escape, nor that we let our avocation supersede our vocation. The principal idea is to keep experiencing a productive life—that we continue to contribute and know a sense of accomplishment.

If we miss the opportunity to grow in the plateau, we end up circling round and round without forward progress. The proper use of plateaus can strengthen us as we begin again. The productive man or woman recognizes that achievement breeds achievement.

Low times give us time to slow down for the next climb.

Reflection: Vicki Hitzges

Motivational Speaker

I chuckled to read that *Fred's* idea of a lull was the time-period after a friend sold his company. *My* recollection of a lull was starting a speaking career in my home office with no customers, no paycheck, no leads, no idea of how to begin and no good answer to the question, "What do *you* do?" The truthful answer was, "I make lists and then stop to eat ice cream. I'm quite accomplished at it." *That's* a lull.

When we hit a lull, the principle of inertia takes over. That's the principle that states that people in motion remain in motion, while people who stay in their pajamas until afternoon tend to stay in their pajamas until bedtime. It's a law of physics. When we have a lull, we exhibit the passion of beached trout.

It *is* possible to switch sides—that is, to go from sitter-quitter to mover-shaker. However, it's difficult. That's because lethargy infects us with depression. Depressed people don't want to go and do—we want to stop and plop. We want to sleep, watch TV and eat. Working out or getting involved gets less appealing as each day slides past. Bad habits take over quickly, like a net dropped on us as we go about our slothful ways. As the lethargy continues, the depression only continues to deepen. It clamps on like Mike Tyson to an opponent's ear.

When we produce, however, our spirits rise. Anne Frank noted, "Laziness may appear attractive, but work gives satisfaction."

Or as Zig Ziglar stated it, "Happiness is something to do."

Former Prime Minister Margaret Thatcher observed, "Look at a day when you are supremely satisfied at the end. It's not a day when you lounge around doing nothing; it's when you've everything to do, and you've done it."

Three Questions to Think About

1. In what area of my life besides work do I satisfy my need for accomplishment?
2. If I lost my job, what would be left to define me?
3. How can I create productive outlets in my life?

One Line to Remember

Low times give us time to slow down for the next climb.

Scripture to Hide in Your Heart

So I recommend the enjoyment of life, for there is nothing better on earth for a person to do except to eat, drink, and enjoy life. So joy will accompany him in his toil during the days of his life which God gives him on earth (Ecclesiastes 8:15).

21

RESPONDING TO THE ALMIGHTY

Fred's Observation

Someone asked me to define "joy of the Lord." I think of it in four words: "awe," "praise," "thanksgiving" and "obedience."

When I feel the *awe* of God, I feel His reality. For example, when I think of the mind that created our DNA, I am in awe. Watson and Crick received the Nobel Prize for identifying God's work. Think of the intellect and the vocabulary needed to determine the number of stars and then call them all by name. I am astounded.

He is worthy of our *praise*, and when I lift up His name, I am acknowledging His worthiness. I praise Him for His common grace to all. I praise Him for who He is. Praise gives me the experience of His presence.

Thanksgiving, to me, is more personal. It is not just giving assent to His worthiness but also giving an offering for His manifold blessings. In thanksgiving, I magnify His name for all that He has done for me as an individual. Through our personal relationship, I feel His presence.

Certainly in *obedience* I acknowledge His authority and know His presence. When I respect the traffic laws, I am recognizing that I am in the presence of civil authority. When I obey scriptural mandates, I am recognizing that I am in the presence of God. I acknowledge the presence of Him who gave all law when I bow my knee to His authority.

Brother Lawrence said, "There is not in the world a kind of life more sweet and delightful than that of a continual conversation with God. Those only can comprehend it who practice it and experience it."

I experience the presence of God in the reality of awe, the worthiness of praise, the offering of thanksgiving and the acknowledgment of obedience. In these we find joy.

Reflection: Donald Campbell

Former Professor and President, Dallas Theological Seminary
Dallas, Texas

Fred writes of experiencing the presence of God through *awe, praise, thanksgiving* and *obedience.* The contemplation of these themes took me to that most wonderful portion of Scripture, the psalms.

The exuberant language of Psalm 19 expresses the worshipful *awe* of David. The message is clear—this awesome God did not leave us in the dark. He communicates to all people everywhere through nature and through Scripture. God's revelation came to us through the Big Book (the universe) and the Little Book (the Bible).

The language of *praise* is found in Psalm 8, a perfect example, says one author, of what a hymn should be: a celebration of God for His glory and grace. The psalm begins and ends with God: "O Lord, our Lord, how majestic is your name in all the earth" (v. 9, *NIV*).

Nowhere in Scripture is the virtue of *thanksgiving* more elegantly expressed than in the well-known Psalm 103. One pastor suggested that David lists his blessings lest in some dark, depressing moment he should forget God and take

His grace for granted. David may have written this psalm in his later years, when he had a clearer sense of the frailty of life, a keener sense of sin and a higher sense of the blessing of forgiveness. As such, this is a psalm that will minister to us over a lifetime.

The theme *obedience* receives scant attention in the Psalter, save for the plaintive divine comment, "But my people did not obey me; Israel did not submit to me" (Psalm 81:11). Of course, people today face the same choice—will it be obedience or disobedience, belief or unbelief?

Thank you, Fred, for stimulating us to think again on these great biblical truths that enable us also to experience God's presence.

Three Questions to Think About

1. What is the theme of my conversations with God?
2. How do awe, praise, thanksgiving and obedience influence my life?
3. What are the "big book" and the "little book" teaching me?

One Line to Remember

When I feel the awe of God, I feel His reality.

Scripture to Hide in Your Heart

The heavens declare the glory of God, the sky displays his handiwork. Day after day it speaks out, night after night it reveals his greatness (Psalm 19:1-2).

22

FISCAL FIDELITY

Fred's Observation

The truth about money has been known for a long time. Aristotle called it "barren"—not because it doesn't bring benefits, but because the emotions it evokes are among the lowest on his hierarchy of values. The feelings invoked by money just don't compare with the nobler emotions of love, patriotism and religion. The man or woman whose greatest emotional energy is reserved for money knows nothing of the higher emotional life.

Money can bring fun—even happiness—but not joy, if it is only money for money's sake. It has no intrinsic ability to elevate the intellect or spirit. In fact, the love of gold often blocks the love for all else that is higher and nobler. How pale the struggle for wealth becomes when compared to the struggle for freedom, the search for truth, the war for principles or the fulfillment of the nobler passions.

However, money is one of life's greatest necessities. To disparage money per se is to demonstrate an ignorance of life and its "rules." I often say that I think about money like I think about blood. I make blood to live—I don't live to make blood. The same thing is true for me about money. I make money to live, but I certainly don't live to make money.

In my view, money has always represented *option*. I have been poor and I have been financially comfortable—I prefer the latter. But having money and loving money are poles apart.

The options that money make possible are part of its utility. Without it, there are limited choices; with it, choices are opened up. The interesting thing about money and choices is that having many options don't necessarily mean that we have the ability to use them well. Therefore, money requires discipline, as do the decisions that money makes possible.

Reflection: Curtis Meadows

Authority on Philanthropy and Family Foundations
Former President, Meadows Foundation, Dallas, Texas

When I talk to groups about money, I usually ask them a series of questions, hoping that they will see that money is a lot more than the number on the balance sheet. Fred makes me think about many of those questions. Here are just a few.

1. What are some words or phrases that describe the concept of money and its accumulation to you (purchasing power, capacity, security, freedom, control, ownership)? Humorist Vic Oliver once observed, "If a man runs after money, he's money-mad. If he keeps it, he's a capitalist. If he spends it, he's a playboy. If he doesn't get it, he's a ne'er-do-well. If he doesn't try to get it, he lacks ambition. If he gets it without working for it, he's a parasite, and if he accumulates it after a lifetime of hard work, people call him a fool who never got anything out of life."

2. What are some of the advantages of having money?

3. What are some of the disadvantages?

4. Does it make life better for our families?

5. Does it create problems for our families *with others*? Theodore Roosevelt one said, "Probably the greatest harm done by vast wealth is the harm that we of moderate means do ourselves when we let the vices of envy and hatred enter deep into our own natures."

7. What are some of the good things we can do with money?

8. What are some of the not-so-good things we can do with money?

Jesus spoke of the difficulty of reconciling all that comes with wealth and living the life Christians are called to when He challenged the wealthy young ruler with the price of following Him. When wealth is used in helping others more than helping ourselves, it can be a powerful impelling force toward significance. When it is used to insulate and isolate us, we will have trouble hearing the voice of Jesus or the cries of pain from a sinful world.

Three Questions to Think About

1. Why is the love of money a root of corruption?
2. How can I make sure that I make money to live and not live to make money?
3. What are the appropriate uses of money for me, my family and my community?

One Line to Remember

Money can bring fun—even happiness—but not joy, if it is only money for money's sake.

Scripture to Hide in Your Heart

The one who loves money will never be satisfied with money; he who loves wealth will never be satisfied with his income. This also is futile (Ecclesiastes 5:10).

23

VIEWING OUR VALUES

Fred's Observation

The simple life is balanced. It is not necessarily devoid of tensions, but the stresses are balanced. The wife of my good friend John Bullock used to say that she always wanted him to have two irritations at a time because, while having one drove him crazy, with two he could oscillate between them and keep his balance. She was a wise woman!

If our core values were manifested physically, we could see the grotesqueness of imbalance. Years ago I saw a man with elephantitis. It was hard not to notice his distorted features. I started thinking about the impact on people if we wore our value systems externally and others could see a tangible representation of who we are internally. What would a man given over to greed look like? How difficult would it be for others to look past the deformed extremity? What would your value distortion look like?

Great sculpture has to be balanced. Skilled artists can look at a mass of stone or clay and see where the center of gravity is—where the balance exists. A mistake can result in destruction of that balance—and artistic disaster. Purpose is shown through the balanced life, just as the purpose of the artist's material is displayed through his perfected work.

Remember the great story of the statue of David? When Michaelangelo was asked how he carved such a splendid work out of the massive piece of marble, he replied, "Simple.

I just cut away everything that wasn't David." A simple life has cut away everything that isn't real to reveal true purpose. It is beautiful because it is balanced.

Reflection: Richard Allen Farmer

Musician, Evangelist, Teacher, Writer and President, RAF Ministries

Balance. It is a goal for all of us. I have not met a person who states as his or her goal, "I would like to be unstable."

Dean Kamen is an inventor who tinkers in order to solve problems. He invented the portable dialysis machine because he thought people with renal failure should not have to be tethered to a hospital treatment facility. He invented the first drug-infusion pump because he did not think it efficient for nurses to administer precise doses when a machine could do it. Kamen invented the iBOT wheelchair because the sight of a person in a wheelchair struggling to get up a curb or being spoken down to offended Kamen as an engineer and a human being. The wheelchair he invented climbs stairs and rises so that the person in the chair can have an eye-level conversation.

My favorite Kamen invention is the Segway Human Transporter. It is a self-balancing people mover. Through this invention, Kamen addressed the imbalance of which Fred Smith speaks. Who among us is interested in regularly falling down and never getting up again? What makes the Segway work is that it has several gyros in it that override the tendency of the machine to fall.

Likewise, you and I have internal gyros to compensate for our imbalance. Without our internal gyros, we would not be able to stand. There is something in us that keeps us from falling. Biologically, we have been wired to stand rather than to fall. Morally, we make decisions that enable us to stand with integrity and righteousness. Philosophically, we embrace values and truths that virtually guarantee stability.

Fred is right: The simple life is balanced. The tensions that attend us simply because we are human are not ultimate. Now unto Him that is able to keep us from falling.

Three Questions to Think About

1. Can I recognize value distortions in my character?
2. What do equilibrium and balance look like for me?
3. How would I identify my personal gyros?

One Line to Remember

A simple life has cut away everything that isn't real to reveal true purpose. It is beautiful because it is balanced.

Scripture to Hide in Your Heart

Now to the one who is able to keep you from falling, and to cause you to stand, rejoicing, without blemish before his glorious presence (Jude 1:24).

24

BEING USED BY GOD

Fred's Observation

I met Torrey Johnson when he was a young man first starting Youth for Christ. At that time, I was asking certain people I admired for their picture and autograph. He gave me his with the inscription: "To Fred, God's man in God's place." I never felt I could hang that on the wall. I kept it in the desk drawer. I was always condemned by how seldom I felt that I was truly God's man in God's place.

During the times I felt that God was using me, I felt extremely small and extremely secure. When I felt big, I felt insecure because I was depending on my own strength.

Recently when I asked a friend the usual question, "How's it going?" he answered in the best possible way. He said, "Fred, I feel God is using me as I use my time to do the things that He wants done. It doesn't get any better than this!" What a wonderful feeling to realize God is using us rather than our using God. So long as we keep that spiritual dimension in our leadership, people will see God in us.

A great many people want to use God as a credit reference. They include their church work in their biography so that people will think them honest or reliable. They put fish on their business cards and their car bumpers, leading others to believe they are more trustworthy than most. Unfortunately, they can be relied upon to use God, but can God rely on them to be used?

Growing up we sang an old gospel song with the line, "I am satisfied with Jesus," but the question comes to me, "Is Jesus satisfied with me?" When God is using us, He is satisfied.

Reflection: Greg Noland

Grandson of Fred Smith, Sr. and Son of Mary Helen and I. Smith Noland
2007 PhD Recipient, Johns Hopkins University

As Grandfather confesses, I suspect that we are all plagued with questions of inadequacy at one time or another. I believe Moses spoke for all of us by muttering, "Who am I?" when God first called him (see Exodus 3:11). Yet God calls great leaders for a purpose, and He intends to see His will accomplished through His servants.

What was God's response to Moses? Was it a morale-boosting pep talk, one that reassured Moses that he was the ideal man for the job? No, God simply answered, "I will be with you" (see v. 12). It's not about Moses. It's about God! His answer reassures us that we will succeed not because of who we are or who we're not, but because of who He is.

This provides the perfect antidote to our feelings of inadequacy as well as our inclinations to conceit. During such times we should focus not on ourselves, but be reminded of God's presence in our lives—a presence that ensures we will always be in God's place.

Three Questions to Think About

1. What excuses have I used when God has called me?
2. How do I feel inadequate to do God's work?
3. What is stopping me from being used right now?

One Line to Remember

What a wonderful feeling to realize God is using us rather than our using God.

Scripture to Hide in Your Heart

I heard the voice of the sovereign master say, "Whom will I send? Who will go on our behalf?" I answered, "Here am I, send me!" (Isaiah 6:8).

25

TRIBULATION'S PAYDAY

Fred's Observation

Until I spent several months on my back, unable to move, I didn't really appreciate patience. Perhaps I could have given you "three points of managing a patient attitude," but I didn't experientially understand. Now I know that true patience reduces unhealthy distress without diminishing healthy stress. Patience brings poise to our life, enabling us to discern between the important and the less important. It gives us tolerance for the point of view of others. Patience promotes meditation. The Scripture confirms the ancient saint's belief that patience develops character. "Tribulation brings about perseverance and perseverance, proven character and proven character, hope" is the way that Paul said it (Romans 5:3-4, *NASB*). Here we see that hope is in the direct line of blessing with tribulation and patience.

Brother Lawrence said that he prayed for tribulation in order to become stronger so that he might endure even more tribulation. He saw suffering as "God's gymnasium." When you are an A-type personality, everything has to happen quickly. Yet tribulation has its own pace. I have found patience to be the only antidote for my frustrations, most of which have been seated in my ego. I have wanted my own way. Today my immobility and total dependence on others have made patience so valuable in avoiding frustration.

Tribulation can be either positive or negative. The choice is yours to make and as you want it, so it shall be.

Patience, like many of our most valued qualities, is slow growing. Patience is an oak tree, not a cornstalk. Patience is available to all of us who are willing to pay the price: It is not an inherited quality that comes in the genes—it is the result of tribulation and our disciplined response.

Sweating it out in God's gymnasium is hard work, but the Coach knows best.

Reflection: Jack Turpin

President, HallMark Energy, LLC
Christian Layman

A generally accepted trait of our current culture is a keen desire for instant gratification. To what degree we exercise this trait is a direct indication of the development of our patience.

Patience is a God-given quality of character—an integral part of integrity.

Patience is a fruit of the Spirit. When we accept Jesus Christ as our Lord and Savior, our new Helper, the Holy Spirit, brings to us a seed of patience, but we must cultivate it. It must be nurtured and developed. To quote from the great American author and educator Noah Webster, "Patience may spring from Christian submission to the divine will."

Each day I pray to God, "Please give me the patience to live with what I cannot change; please give me the courage to change what I can change; and please give me the wisdom to know the difference."

Having experienced extreme grief with the unexpected death of my wife, I have found dependence and patience absolutely essential to get me through each day—dependence on our Lord, our family, our friends, and patience to allow time for our Lord to help, as I await God's will.

Desiring and having the capacity to listen to others, especially to our loved ones, is a direct indication of the development of our patience.

Patience should not be confused with hesitancy or lack of ability to make decisions. Patience should not be confused with lack of interest or apathy.

The ultimate demonstration of patience is biblically based Christlike living in anticipation of our eternal life with Jesus Christ and our precious loved ones. Strong motivation for such patience develops as we become more familiar with heaven, eternity, the new heaven and the new earth from Bible study.

Three Questions to Think About

1. What creates frustration in me?
2. Am I praying for patience, knowing that tribulations will come?
3. What circumstances demand extreme patience at home, at work?

One Line to Remember

True patience reduces unhealthy stress without diminishing healthy stress.

Scripture to Hide in Your Heart

We also rejoice in sufferings, knowing that suffering produces endurance, and endurance, character, and character, hope (Romans 5:2-3).

26

STANDING STRONG

Fred's Observation

Frankly, I was surprised to find in my study that loyalty is one of the key elements in love. I had always thought of spontaneity and extravagance as characteristic, but now I must add loyalty. As I have recalled personal experiences, it has become much clearer.

For example, when I was near death in the hospital, I woke to see a sign on the wall with just four initials on it: "YTCO." Our granddaughter, Catherine, recalled a story that is very familiar to our family and had made the sign for me. Confederate Cavalry Commander Jeb Stuart always closed his letters to General Robert E. Lee with the words "Yours to Count On" (YTCO). It has become a family motto. Every time I looked up from my bed, I could see those letters and knew that she was saying, "We are with you, Grandfather. We love you."

I am a connoisseur of donut shops. I have sampled them nationwide. In Grand Saline, Texas, I was visiting one of the best and across from me sat a country couple. She wore the gingham and he wore the overalls. Finishing before me, he got up to pay but she didn't get up, which surprised me. Then he came back and bent over to pick her up. I realized that she was in a full body brace. He took her to their pickup truck while all of us watched through the shop's front window. The waitress stood there at the counter and remarked, "He took his vows seriously, didn't he, Mister?"

God's love is evidenced through His loyalty to us. "I will never leave you nor forsake you" (see Deuteronomy 31:6). Our names are engraved on the palms of His hand—permanently. Nothing can separate us from the love of God (see Romans 8:38).

Reflection: Fred Smith

Son of Fred Smith, Sr.
President, The Gathering

When I think about what Dad has taught me about loyalty, I remember a particular experience. Several years ago, my wife, Carol, and I spent time in San Francisco and took a day to hike around the John Muir Woods. We were fortunate to have picked a morning when very few people were there, with no lines or noise. If you've been in the redwood forest, you'll know it's like entering Notre Dame or another of the great European churches. The people are reverent in their respect for these giants from another age. Everyone instinctively looks up! The realization of being in the presence of Earth's oldest living species is overwhelming. Reaching 300 feet in height and with diameters up to 44 feet, these figures of age and beauty have lived up to 2,000 years.

Not knowing anything, I dropped in on a tour just in time to hear the guide describing the remarkable root system of the Muir redwoods. I heard these trees do not grow like pines or oaks with individual root systems. Rather, their root systems, while relatively shallow, are completely interconnected. The trees themselves are all outgrowths of a parent tree and they grow around the parent in a complete circle. That circle is called a "cathedral." One of the keys to their survival is their ability to hold each other up with these merged roots. No known wind can topple them. Virtually no disease can kill them. They thrive in fires. They are knit together inextricably and bound together in the longest living family on record.

That will always be my image of loyalty. It is not just support from a distance or a noble feeling. It is the realization that we are bound up together for life and woven together through our roots that hold us all up through everything that comes.

Three Questions to Think About

1. How do I make sure that I am loyal in my love?
2. What defines loyalty for me?
3. Where do I see God's loving loyalty in my life?

One Line to Remember

God's love is evidenced through His loyalty to us.

Scripture to Hide in Your Heart

For I am convinced that neither death, nor life, nor angels, nor heavenly rulers, nor things that are present, nor things to come, nor powers, nor height, nor depth, nor anything else in creation will be able to separate us from the love of God in Christ Jesus our Lord (Romans 8:38-39).

27

ENTERING THE THRONE ROOM

Fred's Observation

Prayer is both marvelous and mysterious. How marvelous that a sinner saved by grace can at any time commune with the Lord Almighty, Creator of heaven and earth. In the night when I awake and am tempted by frustration, it is so comforting to be able to talk to the Lord about it.

I am not alone in my experience. One of the psychiatrists who helped select the first astronauts told me how they tested them in total isolation to see how much they could withstand. He said some could go indefinitely, and when they examined them, they found that they were the ones who could pray. If we would only realize our opportunity for direct communication with the Lord, how much more we would do it.

I have found that expressing gratitude to God gives me great satisfaction. Surprisingly, I have found it has increased my self-respect. It is so much better to live with a grateful person than with a complainer.

Mysterious is the nature of intercessory prayer. How can my request improve on God's love for others? Yet we are instructed in Scripture to pray for one another, and realistically I would be frustrated if I could not pray for others when there is nothing else I can do for them. Often people will say to me, "At least I can pray for you." I want to remind them that praying is the *most* that they can do for me.

Further, I have never felt that the number of people praying is the vital point. I do not think that God is a politician who is swayed by the numbers. I do not believe that God is impressed with celebrity Christian's prayers any more than He is with those of devout souls living through the hardships and deprivations of life. I would rather have some widow who had a direct line to God praying for me than some famous TV Christian.

When we say, "I am praying for you," we are part of the community of the committed. We are joining hands around the throne to enter into His marvelous and mysterious presence.

Reflection: Seth C. Macon

Senior Vice President in Charge of Marketing (Retired), Jefferson Standard Life Insurance Company

I believe Fred's thoughts on prayer are right on target. After more than 50 years of association with Fred, I have learned to listen carefully to what he says. I, too, wake up at night and feel the need to take it to the Lord in prayer. Prayer is not just asking God for something I desire—even if it is the well-being of a friend or loved one—it is also getting my life, my thoughts, my desires and my actions in tune with the will of God.

We are to love our God with all of our heart and mind, and love our neighbor as ourselves. Prayer is a way to help us accomplish that command. Prayer is a way to express our love for God and also a way to express our love for others.

With new technical developments in communications and transportation, it is easier now to accept the idea that our world is getting smaller and that "our neighbors" really are people throughout the world. We must pray for world leaders and needy people everywhere. Then we must act.

Yes, Fred, I agree prayer is marvelous and mysterious. I don't always understand how it works, but it is the greatest thing we can do for ourselves and for those we love. We must continue to pray for each other.

Three Questions to Think About

1. How do I define prayer?
2. For whom am I currently interceding?
3. What items and people are on my prayer list?

One Line to Remember

When we say "I am praying for you," we are part of the community of the committed.

Scripture to Hide in Your Heart

We thank God always for all of you as we mention you constantly in our prayers (1 Thessalonians 1:2).

28

FUNDAMENTAL PEOPLE PRINCIPLES

Fred's Observation

Here are three simple things that I have learned about people.

First, I have learned that I waste time in trying to correct other people's mistakes. I should use the time to utilize their strengths and buttress their weaknesses. A lot of training programs I have seen are geared to overcoming weaknesses—what a waste of time!

Second, I have learned that you can't change anybody else. Each person has to change himself or herself—you can't do it for them. You can set up pressures or you can be there to encourage, but the action can't be taken for another. You might even create fear that will cause a temporary change but nothing permanent. We spend an awful lot of time putting temporary situations in place, thinking that we have changed a person, but in the end it is only a short-term fix.

Third, I have learned that people are the way they are because they want to be that way. I haven't always believed this. In fact, when I started out in life, I wanted to be a social worker and I became extremely disillusioned with people. Now I am totally convinced that each of us is the way we are because we want to be that way. We rationalize and give all kinds of reasons that it's not true, but bottom line: You are choosing to be who you are.

When you have an opportunity to change and you don't take it, you are deciding to stay where you are. And of course, when you grow through personal challenges, you are becoming who you want to be. People who want to change make a plan. Too often lack of a plan is an easy way to rationalize the unwillingness to make changes.

Reflection: Randy Samelson
President, Contrarian Investors, LLC
President, Counsel & Capital

Before calling Fred, even if it is just to say "hello," I make sure paper and pencil are nearby. After hearing Fred's Observation, I summarized it as follows: "People do not change. Therefore, wisdom requires capitalizing on their strengths and buttressing weaknesses." I then applied his principle in three areas of my life.

As an investor, I have made this principle a central component of my investing philosophy. I recognize that markets are moved by the collective actions of large numbers of people. Occasionally, emotions take control and prices rise and fall dramatically. The pundits are often quick to explain why it is a "new era" or why it is "different this time." For investors who believe people do not change, these words remind me to ignore the pundits and invest accordingly.

As a manager, I find it difficult to consistently apply Fred's Observation. The self-proclaimed "professional problem solver" in me wants to react by fixing people's problems by trying to fix people. However, I cannot think of one single success. The only issue is, when will I recognize my mistake—and stop? (Interestingly, when managing myself, I have increasingly restricted my own activities to one or two strengths—

everything else gets delegated or waits until someone else who is skilled can take charge.)

As a father, I apply the principle, at best, imperfectly. I help my children identify their strengths and passions and then find ways to empower them. However, my professional problem-solving personality is lurking in the anteroom, always willing to fix them.

The bottom line is, absent God's intervention, people do not change. People can progress, but typically only when the power of pain overwhelms the harness of habit. However, habit is extraordinarily potent. Ask the alcoholic or the drug addict or me. Consequently, to minimize my own pain and truly serve others, utilizing strengths and buttressing weakness is the way of wisdom.

Three Questions to Think About

1. How am I choosing to stay stuck in life?
2. What is the best choice that I have made in the last six months?
3. Who is my mentor, or coach?

One Line to Remember

Too often lack of a plan is an easy way to rationalize the unwillingness to make changes.

Scripture to Hide in Your Heart

Therefore encourage one another and build up each other, just as you are in fact doing (1 Thessalonians 5:11).

29

THE BLOOD OF LIFE

Fred's Observation

Sometimes you keep stories to yourself because they are very personal. Sometimes the deep satisfaction that they reflect keeps them private. This is a story out of my early manhood that I have never told before, simply because it was both personal and a very satisfying experience. It didn't need any broadcasting.

When I was a young man in the life insurance business, I went into a lawyer's office where he and his daughter practiced together. As I spoke to them, they were obviously upset and asked me what my blood type was. Although it was a very strange question, I knew that they earnestly needed my answer. When I told him, he said, "That is exactly what we need." And then he continued, "My brother is dying in St. Thomas Hospital and must have blood immediately. Will you give him some of yours?" I was happy to oblige.

We immediately got into the car and headed out. Without doing anything other than taking off my coat, I lay down on a cot beside the man, and they transferred the blood directly from me to him because his need was that urgent. He lived and was very grateful for the transfusion, and once he even mentioned that he would happily pay me. But he saw that his gratitude was enough for me and financial payment would be inappropriate. I never saw him again, but the experience produced total satisfaction.

When our souls were in need of a donation for our salvation, Christ shed His blood. When our souls were perishing, Christ provided a way for eternal life. Christ gave us something that we cannot buy—we can only receive it by faith—namely, His grace. "Would you be free from the burdens of sin? There's power in the blood!"

Reflection: Peter McNally

Managing Director, CMO Partners

What a powerful metaphor God has given us in this story: Fred being delighted to stop what he was doing that day and give his blood, receiving nothing material in return, yet being fully satisfied. A man near death. The urgency of the need. None of the usual preparation. Lie on the cot now, and we are going to connect you. The essential gift for human life . . . blood.

As followers of Christ, we have all been blessed with a complete transfusion—a spiritual transfusion. And for me, the day begins with my quiet time, reading the Word, praying Scripture back to God and reflecting on His claims on my life—because He shed His blood. And this personal discipline of starting the day with Scripture and prayer—alone—is very much like getting a transfusion. But of course, it is a spiritual transfusion. Since I heard this story, I now have this mental image every morning in my quiet time of being hooked up by a line to my Lord and Savior. While this is a mental image, it is completely rooted in the reality that the Son of God shed His blood for me.

I have found that this seemingly simple practice, starting each day with quiet time, makes a huge difference in how

God is able to use me to His glory. On occasion, we may find we need actual blood. But every day, we need the spiritual transfusion. And it is every bit as urgent and necessary as getting blood, if God is going to use us.

So every morning, roll up your sleeve, and invite the Lord to lie down next to you and accept the gift . . . of His love and His blood. It really is a matter of life and death.

Three Questions to Think About

1. What does "the blood of Christ" really mean to me?
2. Who has benefited from my own spiritual transfusion?
3. Where am I putting the power in the Blood to work—at home, church, work?

One Line to Remember

When our souls were in need of a donation for our salvation, Christ shed His blood.

Scripture to Hide in Your Heart

But if we walk in the light as he himself is in the light, we have fellowship with one another and the blood of Jesus his Son cleanses us from all sin (1 John 1:7).

30

MAKING GOOD DECISIONS

Fred's Observation

Our life is a network of decisions. A few are vital, but many are less important. For example, the choice of spouse and the decision to have children are two of the most critical decisions you can make. Buying a new suit is less important—unless you make a major fashion faux pas. An impertinent waitress once said to me, "I see you dressed yourself this morning!"

Decision-making is both an art and a science. There are individuals who intuitively make good decisions, both in seeing problems and possibilities. Kettering, the automotive genius, said, "A problem well-defined is half solved." Others have said, "The secret of good decisions is in knowing all the options." Once we know the options, it is fairly simple to choose the best one.

Before President of Ford Motor Company Robert McNamara would accept someone's suggestion, he would ask, "What other possibilities did you reject in order to accept this one?" Many times the individual would have to admit that the one being presented was the first one considered. McNamara would then insist on other options.

In order to pick good options, you first have to know what the object of the decision is—what it is supposed to solve, either as a problem or as a possibility. I try to first determine the current reality by establishing the current facts—not what I wish they were, but what they actually are. Then I think about the ramifications of each option. Next I think about how each option can be implemented and enforced, since a solution that cannot be executed is totally impractical. In business I have seen some policies that were totally unenforceable, which made the management look weak. A good decision is structurally sound and effectively executed.

Becoming a good decision-maker is a satisfactory experience.

Reflection: John Gillespie

Executive Director, Roaring Lambs

Historians tell us that General Robert E. Lee continually asked his subordinates, "What opportunities do we have before us?" He asked this question of them even up to and including the day of his surrender at Appomattox.

A realistic look at all the opportunities and the ramifications of each possibility helps a leader make good decisions. Yes, Robert E. Lee lost the Civil War, but he made many great strategic decisions, including the one to surrender. But what does this have to do with good decision-making in 2006?

Probably one of the best examples of decision-making was played out Sunday, February 5, 2006, when approximately 134 million of us tuned in to Super Bowl XL. Corporate sponsors invested a whopping $2.5 million per 30-second ad for the opportunity to influence our buying decisions. Would we buy their brand of pizza, tacos, beer, hot sauce or automobile? These corporate sponsors believed we would. Yes, they had visited all the possibilities and determined that Super Bowl advertising was a good decision.

Advertising agencies have been hired to skillfully craft structurally sound advertisements to bring about the corporate sponsors' desired results of *increased sales*. Highly trained staffs have been mobilized to deal with the increased sales. Only time will tell if the investment of financial resources and plan of execution was a good decision. Oh, yes—we were all watching!

It is exciting to wonder, if Robert E. Lee and Robert McNamara were corporate leaders in 2006, would they have considered it a good decision to advertise on the Super Bowl? I don't know. But I do believe that if they were both executives at Ford Motor Company, today we would probably all be driving Fords.

Three Questions to Think About

1. What opportunities do I have before me right now?
2. How do I determine what my options are?
3. Who is a great decision-maker that I respect?

One Line to Remember

Life is a network of decisions.

Scripture to Hide in Your Heart

Choose today whom you will worship . . . I and my family will worship the Lord! (Joshua 24:15).

31

THE WISE READER

Fred's Observation

In a book I read recently, the author says that some people get to age 35 or 40 and then level off in terms of their personal accomplishments, never climbing any higher. He said that during the younger part of your life, just being alive is enough to drive you forward, but then that energy starts to wane. Unless you have a spiritual urge to drive you forward, the physical runs out and you peak. The nonphysical urge that drives you forward is the thing that is the great motivation.

One of the sources of motivation for me is reading. We can't keep up without it. Let me ask you, What do you read? Do you read objectively, for yourself? Do you say, "What do I need to read to improve me?" Until you do, you miss the best of reading.

Of course, it is impossible to read everything. I learned a long time ago that my particular interests and gifts are in three areas: theology, philosophy and psychology. I am an eclectic reader and intrigued by ideas, but since I am a slow reader, I concentrate my reading in these three areas. Make clear decisions about what you read and why.

I wear glasses and maybe you do, too. Mine probably cost about the same as yours. Would you trade lenses with me just because I asked you to? Of course not! That would be silly because yours fit you and mine fit me.

Reading works the same way. Are you reading what the boss is reading, or are you reading what fits you? Are you reading a book because someone sent it to you? How about because it is on the best-seller list? You wouldn't wear someone else's glasses—so don't let anyone else pick your books. Understand what your purpose is for reading and carefully discipline your choices.

And always remember, leaders are readers.

Reflection: Joy Lynn Hailey Reed

Director, Center for Excellence in Learning and Teaching, University of Texas at Dallas

For over two years I have jotted down books that Fred quotes during his Saturday morning conversational open houses. I have a robust bibliography. I agree with him that leaders read.

Leaders need to talk to the people they influence, as well as to diverse types of people outside of the leader's circles. Reading gives leaders the opportunity to understand the variety of viewpoints, opinions and experiences others might have.

Reading is a type of conversation. While the writer usually does not hear what we have to say in response to her words, we still talk to her in our minds as we read. Conversely, a writer imagines his audience and carries on the conversation with the reader.

When people who are like us recommend books, we assume that our common interests will ensure our enjoyment of the book. Best-selling reading may help us when it comes to the social currency of being in the know, but it doesn't deepen us.

The main point is that leaders need to choose different kinds of books:

- Books that will stretch the reader
- Books that are written by authors who are kindred spirits with the reader
- Books that are written by people very different from the reader
- Books that inspire the reader
- And finally, books that entertain the reader

Good leaders learn from a diversity of people and experiences. Good leaders *should* browse writings of those with very different backgrounds, experiences and worldviews. Browsing does not require the investment of reading but allows the reader to avoid ideational myopia that comes from reading only what reinforces one's own perspective. In fact, good leaders should read widely and broadly in order to understand their own place in the world and then lead with greater distinction.

Three Questions to Think About

1. What three books have most influenced my thinking?
2. What books am I rereading?
3. How would I start a conversation with my favorite author?

One Line to Remember

Leaders are readers.

Scripture to Hide in Your Heart

Then books were opened, and another book was opened—the book of life (Revelation 20:12).

32

THE PROVIDENCE OF COINCIDENCE

Fred's Observation

I got a call from a men's retreat that I had led for several years on the West Coast. My physical condition kept me from being there in person, so they wanted to set up a phone call allowing me to say a few words and stay connected to the group. (Over the years the members of this particular group and I had become quite close.) But because the retreat was in the mountains, they were having technical difficulties with the telephone service. Even though they had one of the top professional soundmen working on the project, they were unable to access the retreat center's phone lines. Without a line, they couldn't set up the phone system to make the call work.

Just as the technician was saying that it was impossible to make the connection, a man and his son walked in the door. The man worked for the telephone company and was there to attend the conference. They "happened" to drive up in his phone truck and had all the tools and equipment needed to make this work. He even had the spurs to climb up the pole.

The next step was talking to the neighbor to ask her to agree to TV disruption during the phone call. She graciously invited the man and his son in, served them lemonade and even hugged them when they left! Mission accomplished. When they called me, it was clear as a bell from both sides. So many things happened that night against the odds that we just had to give the Lord credit.

Many times events occur in our life that are "beyond arithmetic." The numbers just don't add up. Nonbelievers call these coincidences, but we are happy to see them as evidences of God's active presence in our everyday life.

Reflection: Evelyn Hinds

Actress and Dramatic Interpreter of Corrie ten Boom

Fred explained his term "beyond arithmetic" one Saturday morning to those of us sitting around his bed (during our weekly session of "Fred in the Bed"). I connected right away and sensed his awe of God's timing.

One morning, theologian Ramesh Richard joined the group. I had heard about him from Fred. It was a large group that day, and I decided to maneuver my way through the crowd to meet Dr. Richard at the end of Fred's talk. I wanted to thank Dr. Richard for his writing that had blessed me.

I introduced myself by telling him about my ministry portraying Corrie ten Boom. I knew that he was from India and had a heart to share Christ in the poorest countries in the world. He surprised me by telling me that Corrie had visited his home when he was a child in India in 1961.

When I then told him that I was due to travel to New Delhi in a few days to join my husband, he immediately offered, "I used to be a pastor in New Delhi, and I have a friend who is a pastor there now. They would love to see your presentation." That very day Dr. Richard made arrangements by email for me to present my "Corrie ten Boom Live" on my trip to India.

Although India is a country in which a very small percentage of the people are Christian, the congregation of Delhi Bible Fellowship numbered over 300 members. My husband was already staying at a hotel that was less than two miles from that church. To further my awe at God's timing, the date of my performance coincided with my fifty-fifth birthday. I received God's arithmetic in that instance as an unexpected birthday present!

Three Questions to Think About

1. What do I consider a coincidence that is really God's work?
2. Is God "connecting the dots" in my everyday life?
3. How can I teach my family to look for God's hand at work in our life?

One Line to Remember

Many times events occur in our life that are "beyond arithmetic."

Scripture to Hide in Your Heart

Jesus looked at them and replied, "This is impossible for mere humans, but for God all things are possible" (Matthew 19:26).

33

LEADING BY EXAMPLE

Fred's Observation

Role models personify who we would like to become. My wife, Mary Alice, had three women in her early life who laid out the path she wanted to walk. The first was her high school teacher, Miss Brown. She was stately, dignified and totally ladylike. Mary Alice saw in her what she felt a Southern lady should be. Next was her Bible teacher, Mrs. Keane, who taught a group of young mothers to understand the Scriptures. Her cup overflowed with love and grace from the Lord to those young women. Mary Alice would say, "She is what a Christian should be."

Then there was Miss Gordon, a tiny, immaculately groomed woman in her eighties. She had been raised in wealth but spent a great deal of her time reaching prisoners for Christ. On occasion we would take her to church, and other times we would simply visit. We "sat and warmed our hands in the fire of her love," in Gert Behanna's words. Miss Gordon personified the quiet power of victory. When she died, it was a short step from here to heaven . . . much like Mary Alice's own passing.

Mary Alice found in these three women role models who set a pattern for her adult life. They influenced her not by what they had but by who they were, just as Mary Alice influenced others by her own life.

Observation and *identification* are the important elements in role-model mentoring. Often the role model is not conscious of his or her effect on another. Sometimes there is little personal contact between the two. Sometimes the role model will be a Bible character or a public figure. Often we look to historical men and women as our models.

Role models are a visual embodiment of our personal goals and direction. In them, you can see yourself as you create a pattern for living.

Reflection: Henry Horrell

Businessman and Lifelong friend of Fred Smith, Sr.

My wife and I have experienced the blessing of Fred and Mary Alice's modeling. This poem of mine reminds me of Fred:

Seeing God
I've seen God manifest
In a good friend who is mine
The spirit shown was pure love
This friend is oh so kind.

I saw a flower nod its head
In the breeze that passed it by
Its beauty, fragrance spoke of God
To those who were near by.

A puppy came with wagging tail
Its eyes were filled with love
Again I saw the God I seek
He's here not just above.

Jesus told his followers
If it's God you want to see
Then see the loving thing I've done
You should see God in me.

Now I see God in many things
For love is plain to see
But there's a problem that I have
Do they see God in me?

Three Questions to Think About

1. Whom do I consider my role model?
2. Who is watching me for life clues?
3. What pattern for living will help me achieve my goals?

One Line to Remember

Role models personify who we would like to become.

Scripture to Hide in Your Heart

But as for you, communicate the behavior that goes with sound teaching (Titus 2:1).

34

THE LAST WORD

Fred's Observation

When I was 28, I sat in a cemetery thinking about what I wanted my family to put on my tombstone. "He Stretched Others" came to mind, and it hasn't changed in 63 years.

Recently our son, Fred, asked me, "If you had only one more talk to make, what would be the subject?" Intriguing question, don't you think? As we all face our mortality, we think more seriously about the impact of our speech and our example. We know that our time to influence others is limited. Just as Fred had asked me, I started asking others. I find it a worthy question.

I was then challenged to describe the process of answering the question. "Everyone hasn't thought about these issues as much as you have, Fred. Give me some help on processing my own answer." So here are some questions that I thought about in forming mine.

1. What one fact do I feel has affected my life the most?
2. What one final thing would I say to my children and grandchildren?
3. What is the one statement that most deeply stirs me?
4. What is the one thing that I could say that would affect my hearers the most?

Whether it's one last speech to make, one last song to sing or one last book to write, it makes a difference when you know what your final expression will be. In defining this, you find out a lot about who you are and what your life's purpose is.

(In case you were wondering, my last speech would be "The True Nature of Man." Is man basically good with a tendency toward sin, or basically sinful with a possibility for good? The answer to this question influences all human relationships and commerce.)

Reflection: Haddon Robinson

Harold Ockinga Chair of Distinguished Preaching,
Gordon-Conwell Seminary, South Hamilton, Massachusetts
Author and Radio Personality

Most people who speed read their morning paper completely overlook the most provocative section of all: the obituaries. It takes imagination to read them well. You have to read between the lines and wonder. Most of the column is taken up with standard stuff like who died, the funeral home in charge of the burial, the time of the viewing, and the time and place of the memorial service. The space that remains sums up a life.

Esther Devett had a husband and three children who "survived her." The obituary writer shines the spotlight on the fact that for 23 years, Esther headed up the bridge club in her town and "under her leadership, it expanded to 23 tables." That doesn't seem worthy of a life.

Henry Murlock died at age 93. His wife, Emily, preceded him in death 22 years before. No other family is mentioned, and apparently Henry outlived his friends. Obviously, he didn't have a big funeral. I expected the obituary to say, "Instead of gifts to charity, it is requested that flowers be sent."

Laura Bracalli died at age 69. She was married to the same man for almost 50 years. They had four children, seven grandchildren and two great grandchildren. Her obituary noted, "Laura loved everybody she met, and everyone loved her." I imagine that she had a big funeral and folks were grieved to see her go.

In an obituary notice in a small-town Kansas newspaper, there was the observation, "Lloyd was born again at 37." People in Kansas knew that was important. Evidently, Lloyd was never the same after that.

Jesus reported on the obituary of a farmer who had made it big in agriculture. The farmer had expanded his operation to build more and more barns to store all his crops. He had anticipated retirement when he could kick back and live, but the night his plans were finalized he had a sudden heart attack and died. Jesus called him a fool. If that farmer could have played golf for four more years, do you think Jesus would have changed His verdict?

To think about death too much is morbid. Not to think about it at all is stupid. Sometime soon, take an hour or two and use Fred's questions to write your own obituary. At your death, how do you want your life to be characterized? Are you ordering your life today to make that happen?

Three Questions to Think About

1. What would my final message be?
2. How do I encourage others to consider this important question?
3. What and who really make a difference in my life?

One Line to Remember

Whether it's one last speech to make, one last song to sing or one last book to write, it makes a difference when you know what your final expression will be.

Scripture to Hide in Your Heart

I have competed well; I have finished the race; I have kept the faith! (2 Timothy 4:7).

35

FREE TIME THAT COUNTS

Fred's Observation

Many times our leisure determines whether we are going to be mediocre or successful. A Christian should use leisure constructively to build and not to abuse. Weekend carousal is out. Volunteer work and healthy diversion are positive ins.

Leisure gives us time for reading, studying, traveling and ministering. We are to *invest* our leisure, not *spend* it. I want my leisure time to pay dividends like any other good investment. A good hobby provides relaxation—a bit of spice for life. Recreation should be re-creation. Our pleasures should restore our energy and create pleasant memories.

For many, recreation is the opposite . . . like the nurse sitting in the adjoining seat from Miami to Chicago. I asked her whether she was coming home or going to work. She said that she was returning from a long weekend of partying in the islands. Her eyes looked like two red traffic lights. She was going to have to go home to her job just to recuperate from her leisure! This, certainly, isn't the Christian's way. She had made a big payment for this leisure time without hope of any interest dividend!

My friend Jed Thompson uses his vacation time to work in a boat on the Amazon River, bringing with him dentists and technicians who volunteer their time, as well as dental and medical supplies. They go up and down the area ministering to the local people—first to their health needs and then to their spiritual lack. Another family takes part of their summer vacation to go to the poorest areas in the world to serve Christ. These folks as well as those who participate in church building and Habitat for Humanity understand the true nature of leisure time.

Service to others is a pleasure unknown to the selfish. In William Barclay's prayer he asks for pleasure in his leisure. This only comes through the giving of oneself to something bigger than oneself.

Reflection: Donna Skell

Director of Public Relations, American Tract Society
Speaker and Women's Ministry Leader

The Scriptures tell us to ask God to teach us to number our days aright that we may gain a heart of wisdom (see Psalm 90:12). To become wise, we must spend our time rightly. Whether leisure time is several days, several hours or just a few minutes, there is a best way to utilize that time. I believe that when I ask God how to best use that time, He will direct my path.

Often for me it is to rest my physical body and mind—to place no demands on myself, to empty my mind, to close my eyes, to withdraw from people, to recharge myself physically. Sometimes it is in front of a TV set, although I could not tell you what is on. Sometimes that personal refreshment comes from just the opposite source, as I feel the need to go for a walk or do something physical to energize and release endorphins. That time is always spent dwelling on the Lord, as I listen to praise music and admire the beauty that God has created.

Many times I feel a strong need to give my time to someone else. Sometimes it is a call to encourage, give a listening ear and catch up with someone. Other times it is a handwritten note. Scheduling leisure time for friends is an important part of building relationships. If you have many friends, then you know the time commitment it requires.

I see leisure time as flex time—time that we are given to be flexible to the nudging of God. I believe time is a gift from God that He expects us to give back to Him, to give to others and to use for the betterment of ourselves. I believe it is our job to seek His will for that time, to squeeze the most good from it and to do the things that enable us to live a life pleasing in the sight of our Lord.

Three Questions to Think About

1. How do I spend my leisure time?
2. How can I feel God's pleasure in my leisure time?
3. What allows me to "re-create"?

One Line to Remember

A Christian should use leisure constructively to build and not to abuse.

Scripture to Hide in Your Heart

God finished the work that he had been doing, and he ceased on the seventh day all the work that he had been doing (Genesis 2:2).

36

CONTROLLING THE EGO

Fred's Observation

I remember an embarrassing situation that occurred one night at a business meeting with a group of high-profile executives. One man, who considered himself an authority on international oil because he read the newspaper, was popping off about the energy situation and its easy resolution. Unbeknownst to him, another man in the room had just returned from chairing an international conference of major oil companies. After the first fellow finished spouting off (only proving his ignorance), the second man quietly but effectively exposed him as the fool that he was.

I quickly said to myself, *I hope that never happens to me*! I left that meeting determined to make sure that in my speaking I always remember that someone in the audience may know a lot more about the subject than I do. The memory of that business meeting has stayed in my mind and tempered many remarks I've been tempted to make.

On the other hand, sometimes speakers are too impressed with who's in the audience. One night I was in a church listening to a preacher when I saw a well-known university president slip into the sanctuary. Clearly, the preacher saw him enter as well, for he changed his style considerably. I could tell he was preaching for the benefit of this one individual. He went from preaching to giving an intellectual performance, trying to impress with his learning. He seemed to forget the rest of the audience.

Being impressed with ourselves or with the celebrity of another blocks the power of good communication. In our work and in our speech, we should always remember that God is listening and He is our ultimate audience.

It is never far from my thinking that God is present and if He isn't, we ought to dismiss early.

Reflection: Max Hulse

Retired Stockbroker, Lay Leader, Philanthropist and Artist

Who among us has been so fortunate to avoid both these humiliating experiences? Might we not say that he or she who has been so wise—or lucky—can cast the first stone?

Ego is a human trait that can be a vice or a virtue. An egocentric person may strive to impress others with his or her own intelligence, education or accomplishments, and thus appear boorish or obnoxious.

By contrast, the person with a healthy ego is a pleasant companion. He or she feels no compulsion to impress his or her audience, does not monopolize the conversation and usually is a good listener. This person probably has a good sense of humor. He or she also exudes a calm assurance derived from knowing who he or she is. Further, the person with a healthy ego recognizes his or her strengths and weaknesses, and feels no compulsive need to emphasize either. In my opinion, this is true humility.

Wisdom is a gift from God available to all who will ask. To ask requires a certain amount of humility—which acknowledges that God is God, instead of my being God.

Therefore, it is my contention that wisdom and humility are closely related, and if a person has one of these qualities, he or she probably also has a good measure of the other.

There is an old axiom that is tried and true: *Be yourself!* You may not be the best-looking, most intelligent or most charismatic person, but sincerity, integrity and humility will compensate for shortcomings and shield you from humiliating experiences.

Three Questions to Think About

1. How do I season my speech with grace?
2. What does it take for me to really know myself?
3. Do I listen as well as I should?

One Line to Remember

In our work and in our speech, we should always remember that God is listening and He is our ultimate audience.

Scripture to Hide in Your Heart

The fear of the LORD provides wise instruction, and before honor comes humility (Proverbs 15:33).

37

ANSWERING THE CALL

Fred's Observation

There's a difference between a mandate and a call. A call is personal—it comes to the individual. A mandate is collective. While a call is an individual's reason for service, a mandate is an organization's reason for being.

A leader needs to have a sense of call to serve effectively. Prison evangelist Bill Glass emphasizes this when training his prison counselors. He says, "You have volunteered to be a counselor, but you have dedicated your life to personify Christ in this prison." He goes through a litany of experiences that a volunteer might find offensive but knows that the dedicatees will hang in.

A call may change. A person might sense a calling to a different organization or a different form of service. Sometimes I think the call may actually lead someone out of the ministry. Recently I talked with a pastor in Iowa whose primary ministry was Bible teaching. I asked him how he was doing, and he admitted he was unhappy. So were his people. I asked him, "What is your real love?"

"Winning people to Christ" was his answer.

"In your saint-saturated organization," I said, "there is nobody to win. And whenever you get up to teach, you don't see a single soul who needs salvation. You are by nature an evangelist. Have you considered leaving the ministry and going back into automobile sales, where you are constantly in contact with lost people?"

"That's where I was the happiest," he said.

He had allowed church pressure and his ego to get involved, and he ended up in the pastorate. When I checked back with him, he had gone back into sales—and was happy and effective in his evangelistic efforts.

His call to win people did not match the organization he was serving. Now his call and his passion are in harmony.

Reflection: Mary Helen Noland

Daughter of Fred Smith, Sr.

Director of Admissions, Trinity Christian Academy, Addison, Texas

When Dad says, "a leader needs to have a sense of call to serve effectively," I agree fully. However, there is a sad and dangerous little game people play in the Christian community. It's played out in the church at the highest levels, and it's this whole concept of God's call.

My husband and I have served for a number of years as counselors at Marble Retreat, a secluded hideaway nestled in the mountains of Colorado. We meet clergy couples that come for intensive therapy during or at the bottom of a personal and/or ministry crisis. As we listen to their stories about the call to ministry, it's often not the call of God, but the call of guilt. Some feel saddled with the misplaced expectations of someone else's dream. Unfortunately, within many denominations, the fulfillment of "the call" happens only through ordained ministry. One young pastor remarked angrily, "I am tired of God calling me collect.

Every time He calls, I end up paying."

There is a vast difference between feeling drafted by God and being drawn. I believe that we are called *first* to God—to be forgiven and restored—and then, and only then, can we listen to the voice from within about meaningful life work. In *The Hungering Dark*, Frederick Buechner says:

> The world is full of people who seem to have listened to the wrong voice and are now engaged in life work in which they find no pleasure or purpose and who run the risk of suddenly realizing someday that they have spent the only years that they are ever going to get in this world doing something which could not matter less to themselves or to anyone else. Your calling is the place where your deep gladness and the world's deep hunger meet.[1]

I have a sneaking suspicion that when I discover that deep gladness Buechner talks about, I won't feel drafted but drawn—and to paraphrase Dad, I will know that my call and my passion are in harmony.

Three Questions to Think About

1. Where am I drawn, not drafted?
2. Which areas in my life need harmonizing?
3. How can I help others find their call?

One Line to Remember

There's a difference between a mandate and a call. A call is personal—it comes to the individual. A mandate is collective.

Scripture to Hide in Your Heart

Then the Lord came and stood nearby, calling as he had previously done. "Samuel, Samuel!" Samuel replied, "Speak, for your servant is listening!" (1 Samuel 3:10).

Note

1. Frederick Buechner, *The Hungering Dark* (San Francisco: Harper-SanFrancisco, 1969).

38

FLYING WITH THE EAGLES

Fred's Observation

I believe that I am responsible for my own personal development. Only I know who I want to become. Only I know my real strengths and weaknesses, my passion and my talent. Only I know the price I am willing to pay to be who I can become. My personal development stands on four legs.

The first leg is mentoring. When I was young, I heard the expression, "Birds of a feather flock together." I knew then that I wanted to associate with individuals who would be my mentors and role models. So early in my business career, I chose six qualities that I wanted to build into my life and I asked individuals who personified each to give me an autographed picture. I framed these pictures, along with Hoffman's *Head of Christ at 33* and a mirror. I then hung them on the wall in a circle, with the head of Christ on the top, the mirror on the bottom and the others around. I could look at the pictures and at my reflection and determine whether I was growing in these qualities. This was the first step in my development program.

Reading is the second leg of my development program. I do prescription reading: Just as everyone doesn't have the same eyeglass prescription, not everyone is helped by reading the same thing. I read no novels. I concentrate on certain authors who can give me what I need, such as Chambers,

Fénelon, Drucker and Laubach. I also read individual chapters in books that are focused on my major reading themes: philosophy, theology, mentoring and psychology. These are areas for which I have a natural affinity.

The third leg of my development stool is writing. Until I started working for Maxey Jarman, chairman of Genesco, I was a totally verbal person. Once I was telling him about a situation in the plant and he said, "Write it." When I told him I couldn't write it, he said, "The reason you can't write it is that you don't know it. Anything you know you can write." I later came across the quote from Sir Francis Bacon, "Writing makes an exact man." I learned to write to burn the fuzz off my thinking.

The final leg of my development plan is travel. It opens wide the window of experience and expands my viewpoint.

Personal development is just that—a personal effort with a personal price tag, but without it I would be poor indeed.

Reflection: Charlie "Tremendous" Jones

Author, Life Is Tremendous

"Birds of a feather flock together" is a great truth, and one that goes with it is, "When the student is ready, the teacher will appear." In my youth I was not a reader and my interest was all self. But when I was 22, a friend introduced me to the Bible and the Lord Jesus Christ. I was arrested, convicted and pardoned that day and my whole world changed.

The first Sunday I attended Sunday School as a Christian, they invited me to teach a class of eight-year-old boys. I was totally ignorant of anything spiritual, with the exception of John 3:16 and John 5:24. So the superintendent gave me two books, *What the Bible Is All About* by Henrietta Mears and *Teaching the Truth* by Donald Grey Barnhouse. Because I was ready and willing to learn, God sent me two tremendous teachers in these two books.

That was the beginning of an adventure that has grown more exciting and meaningful over 56 years. My life has been blessed by the lives of many great men, but no personal experience has matched the miracle power of a book. A book you can hold, hug, feel, smell, underline, memorize, realize and even caress. Many of the great men that have shaped my life have been dead many years—men like Chambers, Fénelon, Spurgeon, Tozer and Nee.

Maxey's counsel to "write it" was right as well. I discovered years ago that I don't need self-confidence; I need preparation. I've been forced to write many times and have been grateful because writing makes me think and rethink my thoughts.

Travel is an education and I'm thankful for the many states, provinces and countries I've visited, but I must always turn the spotlight to books. With imagination and good books, you can see the world.

Thank you, Fred, for showing us that we are what we read.

Three Questions to Think About

1. What type of development program am I using?
2. How am I using reading in my development?
3. Who are some authors who have greatly aided my development?

One Line to Remember

Only I know the price I am willing to pay to be who I can become.

Scripture to Hide in Your Heart

They read from the book of God's law, explaining it and imparting insight. Thus the people gained understanding from what was read (Nehemiah 8:8).

39

HOLDING A TAUT LINE

Fred's Observation

Successful leaders have learned to appreciate tension. I am convinced that positive stress is a wonderful thing. Where else would we get the energy to carry out our responsibilities? Botanists teach us about the importance of turgor—that normal fullness that comes from the tension produced by fluid flowing through veins of plants. Lack of proper tension makes plants droop. We are no different. Without a healthy degree of stress and tension, we wilt.

Certainly we must control stress, but we must not eliminate it. One of the finest ways to control it is by learning to appreciate it, rather than fearing it. If you didn't have tension, you wouldn't have enough ambition to become successful.

We had a young man who, when asked the question "How long have you been working for the company?" responded with "Ever since the boss threatened to fire me!" This young man didn't have the eye of the tiger nor the fire in the belly that true leaders need. Successful men and women have an intense rhythm and energetic pace.

I sometimes hear wives complain about how tired their husbands are at night. I think this is part of the price of being a leader. You can't have the placidity of a mule and the winnings of a racehorse!

A psychiatrist friend of mine was sent to Guadalcanal following the bloody battles with the Japanese in 1942 to talk with both the heroes and the cowards to see why each reacted as he did. My friend told me that both were motivated by the same great fear, but the heroes ran forward and the cowards ran backward.

The same thing is true in business. We either face problems as challenges or withdraw into the shell of inertia. We can choose to see obstacles or opportunities.

Reflection: Jim Beckett

President, Beckett Interests

Is it coincidence that Fred is asking me to respond to his thoughts on tension and stress? Me, miraculously revived from a premature and near-fatal heart attack 10 years ago? No, it's just another example of Fred's "provocativity"—his uncanny ability to stimulate his friends and mentees toward positive action by sending them deeper into questioning, seeking and thinking through God's best for their lives, reminiscent of Hebrews 10:24-25.

The way I see it, stress and tension flare up when a difficult decision needs to be made. Statistics, which is my educational background, has been defined as the "science of decision-making in the face of uncertainty."

Rather than running forward or backward, I consider decisions more as a fork in the road, where I can take the high road or the low road—or wait at the intersection for more data. (In the heroic sense, maybe it's fight, flight or freeze.) The high road frequently involves significant short-term cost (or you wouldn't have a tough decision), but it is really the only choice for reducing toxic and debilitating long-term stress. In my life this is evidenced by my poor sleep if I choose the low road or false comfort derived from overstaying in my analytical mode inappropriately, which can actually exacerbate the tension and stress.

I have found that whether I'm facing a tough business or personal decision (and need I say that the personal decisions can be much tougher), having trusted mentors and accountability relationships helps immensely. Usually we can see each other's issues and stress-reducing solutions more clearly than our own. Thanks, Fred, you are the quintessential mentor.

Three Questions to Think About

1. Do I appreciate stress in my life, or do I fear it? Why?
2. What is my thought process when making an important decision?
3. What, if anything, in that process needs to be changed to aid in healthier decision-making?

One Line to Remember

We either face problems as challenges or withdraw into the shell of inertia.

Scripture to Hide in Your Heart

Stay alert, stand firm in the faith, show courage, be strong (1 Corinthians 16:13).

40

THE INTEGRITY OF LEADERSHIP

Fred's Observation

As I think about spiritual leadership, I am convinced that the key is the Holy Spirit's energizing and directing the leader's uniqueness and giftedness by giving him or her a vision that creates a passion. I have never known a lazy or confused leader who was clearly passionate. Oat Willie of Austin, Texas, charged "Onward, through the fog." It works for cartoon characters but fails miserably as a leadership mantra.

For years, I have been writing articles targeted to Christian leaders. I have spoken to groups, large and small. I realize that it is difficult to be a Christian leader in an almost totally secular society whose renewed interest in spirituality is nonbiblical. Christian leaders have lost much of the respect that they once enjoyed. Burnout is common. Depression is almost epidemic. Stress is increasing. Immorality and divorce are more prominent. Short tenure is too much the rule, rather than the exception. More and more preachers are faced with the demand to entertain and excite.

Could a major part of this problem be that leaders have lost their vital identification with the Lord? Have they become convinced they work for the church rather than for God? Are they surrendering their spiritual authority to the church board?

Some in Christian leadership are misplaced. Remember the farmer who read a "GP" in the clouds, immediately left the field and headed for the pulpit? After he failed as a pastor, the word came down from above: "Farmer Brown, 'GP' meant go plow, not go preach!" Leaders who are not endowed with gifts energized by the Spirit become easy prey to human methodology and open themselves to the temptations of power, prestige and money. Christian leaders should always remember that theirs is a calling, not a career. That it's all about stewardship, not ownership. Focus in service brings joy.

Reflection: Jay Kesler

President Emeritus, Taylor University, Upland, Indiana

In the final analysis, and I do mean the *final* analysis, the leader must decide from what source he or she wants to hear the words, "Well done, good and faithful servant." Between today and the judgment, there are many siren songs waiting to seduce the Christian leader to alter his or her original course of looking unto Jesus. Voices clamor for him or her to settle for the lesser rewards of power, money, acclaim or, in the world where I have been living these last 20 years—the academy—the almost irresistible temptation of intellectual respectability and human pride.

As usual, Fred is right: The ideal of servant leadership has been reduced to a method of manipulation and a formula for success. Yet leadership in the Christian sense is "followship" and the leader/example is Christ alone. Testing the spirits is primary. Biblical truth, carefully studied, informed by the lessons of history and guided by the indwelling of the Holy Spirit, is the leader's compass and Christ Himself is the magnetic pole. It is at His throne that the only meaningful pronouncement can be made: "Well done, good and faithful servant." The rest is dross!

Of course, we are warned early on about the dangers of selling our birthright for a bowl of stew. The problem is the same. Our appetites and the hunger of our immediate survival often win out over even our knowledge and spiritual judgment. All the more reason to heed Fred's counsel to stay focused!

Three Questions to Think About

1. How long has it been since I clarified my focus?
2. What is the source of my calling?
3. Where am I possibly out of place?

One Line to Remember

I have never known a lazy or confused leader who was clearly passionate.

Scripture to Hide in Your Heart

He appointed the priests to fulfill their duties and encouraged them to carry out their service in the Lord's temple (2 Chronicles 35:2).

41

THE POWER OF THE PLATEAU

Fred's Observation

Sound development requires a program that provides plateaus in which our information is turned into knowledge through experience and then another climb. Personal growth is not a series of nonstop climbs. Plateaus allow for assimilation before starting the next ascent. Each person has his or her own pattern and must become adept at reading their graph of climbs and plateaus. Those who try to go up too fast either run out of steam or poorly assimilate their experiences. They develop hollow spots.

All of life doesn't evenly and systematically move through the pattern. From a distance, a graphed line may look like a consistent incline. However, when studied up close, the viewer sees that it is a pattern of up, down and flat places. The macro view often looks different from the micro view.

We have natural divisions in our life, such as family, career, spirit, finance, emotions, friends and acquaintances, and physical health. A friend of mine who consults with executives on personal development likens these segments of life to subsidiaries of a corporation. Each one reports to the individual who monitors and supervises the performance of each.

I like to think of the divisions as interrelated but distinct in their focus. Clearly, each has its own particular life cycle of climbs and plateaus. Therefore, it is important to track all areas of our life and keep time tables charted for each area. As we undertake this exercise, we can measure the condition of each division. I do not attempt to have each area in the same mode. Ideally, each has its season for climbs and plateaus. For example, when one is climbing in one's career, energy and positive stress are redirected in that direction. To strive at the same time for climb mode in other areas of life is asking for burnout and poor production.

Understanding the syncopation of life's development rhythm keeps us in sync with progress.

Reflection: John Edmund Haggai

Founder and President, Haggai Institute for Advanced Leadership Training
Author and Lecturer

As I read Fred Smith's ideas—always riveting, always seminal—serendipitous ideas started to tumble over each other in my head.

Moses met God on Mount Sinai. David lifted his eyes unto the hills. Jesus was transfigured on the mountain top. From start to finish, the Scriptures show men and women of faith "going up" to meet God.

Consider also the converse. Satan was cast down from heaven. Adam fell. David passed through the valley of the shadow of death.

Heights of achievement. Depths of despair. And in between?

In between are the plateaus. Progress rarely runs smoothly. A stock price zigzags upward. Climbers ascend Everest by establishing a series of camps on ever-higher shoulders of the mountain. Every leap forward first requires a rest, a regrouping, a regathering of strength.

Sometimes this takes the form of faith-building setbacks.

I think of Joseph, who endured the folly of a doting father, the hostility of jealous brothers, slavery to a band of Midianites, and a prison term for having fled from a vile woman's seduction attempt. Only by means of these successive plateaus did his progress eventuate in the blessing of a top office under Pharaoh.

A plateau is not a plain. In the Bible, the plains often symbolize suffocating luxury and spiritual stagnation: Egypt, Babylon, Sodom and Gomorrah, Shinar—where men built the Tower of Babel.

It's tempting to linger in the level places where the living is easy. But at every plateau, God calls His servants to the next challenge and the next ascent. Onward. And upward.

Three Questions to Think About

1. Where am I right now in the various "subsidiaries" of my life?
2. How do I manage the zigzags of life?
3. What system am I using to track the rhythm of my development?

One Line to Remember

Understanding the syncopation of life's development rhythm keeps us in sync with progress.

Scripture to Hide in Your Heart

So he ran on ahead and climbed up into a sycamore tree to see him, because Jesus was going to pass that way (Luke 19:4).

42

AMPLE AMPS FOR A PRODUCTIVE LIFE

Fred's Observation

We are always warned by the electric company to avoid overloading the circuits. This is right, although I noticed that I have six plugs on one outlet and there is no potential danger because I only use one thing at a time. Each one alone doesn't come close to maxing out the circuitry. We get in overload trouble by using more than one or two—that maxes it out.

The same thing happens in our lives. We get overloaded by having too many demanding involvements, emotional experiences or commitments of time all at once. When we do so, we blow a fuse. It isn't how many connections you have on a circuit; it is how much potential there is for an overload. Sometimes we can take on multiple activities so long as none of them requires too much or is plugged in simultaneously with too many other demands. When they compete for our energy current, we are in danger.

We draw different amounts of current depending on the emotional output required by any particular commitment. I used to speak to very large audiences, and it took practically no energy because the input was matched by the output. If there had been no positive input, such as friendly reactions, laughs, agreements, interest and so on from the audience, it would have taken a great deal more output from me.

You must reach a balance where the amount that you give and the amount that you receive are equivalent—a zero-sum game. We burn out when we are not sharing the energy load in the task, whether intellectual, emotional, physical or spiritual. It is not the number of tasks but the net energy required that determines the point of overload.

Reflection: Bob Deffinbaugh

Pastor/Teacher, Community Bible Chapel, Richardson, Texas

Fred has called our attention to the problem of becoming overloaded with the demands of life and of ministry, the consequence of which has sometimes been referred to as "burnout." I believe that the Scriptures speak to the over-load problem in at least three ways.

First, because we all tend to have too many irons in the fire (or too many appliances plugged into an outlet), we must prioritize these demands and determine that we will seek to accomplish those things that are most crucial first. Martha was too concerned about something that was of lesser importance (see Luke 10:38-42). In short, her priorities were mixed up, so she blew her fuse.

Second, sometimes the solution to overload is simply a matter of plugging a few things into another outlet that is connected to a different circuit. We fix coffee for church and there are too many pots operating at the same time, so we plug them into different circuits. Likewise, we sometimes think we're the only circuit in town. Thus, we believe that we must bear the whole load.

Elijah had this "I alone am left" syndrome, and he nearly burned out. Part of the solution for Elijah was to be informed that he was not alone; indeed, there were 7,000 other faithful servants. God instructed him to appoint three people to get the job done, a job that was never meant for him alone (see 1 Kings 19). In the New Testament, we are taught that the Church is the Body of Christ and that each individual member has his or her role to play (see 1 Corinthians 12:1-31). The point here is that God has distributed the load of ministry among all the members of the whole Body. We need to be careful not to assume the whole load is ours to bear. There are other circuits.

Third, there is also a sense in which God wants us to operate beyond our capacity. God's work is not accomplished by human striving (the flesh) but by God's Spirit at work in us. This was true in the Old Testament (see Zechariah 4:6) just as it is true in the New (see Romans 8:1-11). God gave Paul a "thorn in the flesh" and did not remove it because He wanted him to learn that His power is perfected in weakness (see 2 Corinthians 12:7-10). To pick up on the electrical circuit analogy, God is like an uninterruptible power supply that kicks in when the normal source of power is insufficient.

Three Questions to Think About

1. In what condition is my emotional circuitry?
2. What energy users put me in overload?
3. What part am I playing in sharing the load of the Church?

One Line to Remember

It is not the number of tasks, but the net energy required that determines the point of overload.

Scripture to Hide in Your Heart

"Not by strength and not by power, but by my Spirit," says the Lord who rules over all (Zechariah 4:6).

43

PROTECTED BY LOVE

Fred's Observation

I served on a corporate board with a strong Christian lady who testified that she grew up with friends who lived "on the wild side." Her sister advised her to avoid dangerous behavior, fearing what her father would do to her. She responded, "I am not choosing against immorality because I'm afraid of what he will do to me. But I am choosing because of what it would do to him. I know he truly loves me."

Another friend told how her mother had died when she was a young child. Her relatives told her how much her mother regretted that she wouldn't live to see her daughter grow up. They also told her that her mother lived in heaven and could see everything that she did. Not wanting to disappoint her mother, this woman lived an almost exemplary life. She feared not living up to her mother's love. Children who are loved are less likely to get into serious trouble.

Couples living together without marriage will say, "It's nobody's business what two consenting adults do." This might be true if no one else loved either one of them, but that is rarely the case. Such couples are not living up to the responsibility of being loved.

I once went to Europe with a nonbelieving business associate whom I expected to be a philanderer. But during the entire trip, he only talked of his wife and their love for each other. After attending a concert at La Scala, his only remark was, "I wish she were here." His response to her love became his strength.

I have observed that those individuals who feel Christ's love are eager to obey His commandments. In Scripture it says, "If you love me, you will obey my commandments" (John 14:15). It isn't in obedience that we know Him but we observe His commandments because we know Him. It is our joy.

Reflection: Jill Briscoe

Telling the Truth Ministries
Executive Editor, Just Between Us *Magazine*
Speaker and Author

I am the Christian lady Fred quoted at the beginning of his reflection. I well remember the incident. I was not a believer. A child of the Second World War, I had many questions concerning God and His existence, but I was brought up by parents I adored and who loved and disciplined me. I was also taught Christian values, though we never went to church.

Because I adored my father, I did not want to disappoint him. So when at a high school friend's party I was invited to bed by my boyfriend, I resisted, checked by my big sister's words: "Jill, if you ever get pregnant, it would kill Daddy!" A suitable fear, love and reverence for my father's love saved me in the hour of temptation.

My understanding of the holiness of God and His loving insistence that I be holy has grown since that day! This I have learned is not just for my heavenly Father's benefit but also for mine. God knows sin is a spoiler and ruins our life and the lives of those around us. Because I love Him, I would not willingly break His heart. In fact, the better I know Him, the more intent I am to bring Him joy. Holiness is loving God and obeying Him to that end.

Such intimacy and love require time spent together. When the war was over, I got to know my father and we grew close. He was a fly fisherman, and my sister and I would trek along the rivers with him in the beautiful English Lake District, spending hours in nature's cathedral in silence, just enjoying each other's company. Joy!

So it has been with my heavenly Father. The symphony of silence enjoyed with God my Father alongside the river of life has deepened my love, respect and enjoyment of Him! Obedience without love is a miserable affair. Obedience with love is faith dancing!

Three Questions to Think About

1. Whom do I love enough to obey?
2. How do I develop the right priorities for my time?
3. What tells me today that I am loved by God?

One Line to Remember

It isn't in obedience that we know Him but we observe His commandments because we know Him.

Scripture to Hide in Your Heart

Now this is love: that we walk according to his commandments (2 John 1:6).

44

THE JOY OF NEW IDEAS

Fred's Observation

I asked the senior vice president of a billion-dollar oil company, "John, what do you know now that you wish you had known when you got out of school?"

Very quickly, he responded, "Fred, I wish I had had the humility of an open mind."

Have you ever tried to talk to somebody whose mind is tightly closed?

A common denominator that I have discovered among eager learners is that they are not far from a paper and pen (or any of today's equivalents). Watch for this. Engage highly energetic, ambitious achievers in a stimulating conversation, and suddenly you will see them record an idea that has crossed their mind. Note-taking achievers can throw away their recorded ideas later if they don't want them (and smart folks do evaluate and discard bad ideas). But if they want to remember an idea and haven't jotted it down, how can they recapture it? Howard Hendricks, distinguished professor of Dallas Theological Seminary, has trained thousands of men and women to carry 3x5-inch note cards around to catch "big ideas."

An outstanding young man I recently met said this to me: "A leader is not the one who *has* the best ideas; a leader is the man or woman who *uses* the best ideas." In order to do this, the leader must have an open, discerning mind. Of course,

I am not talking about a sticky flycatcher that picks up everything that passes by, but an astute ability to open up to ideas that are helpful.

I always keep in mind that what leaders know is not uppermost—I am primarily interested in what they are and how they think, for that will determine how well they will use what they know and how they capture that which they don't. Remember, a leader makes friends with his or her ignorance.

Reflection: Mark Bailey

President, Dallas Theological Seminary

In those times when I have had the privilege to be with Fred Smith, I have found him to model the quest for new ideas. The older he grows, the more insatiable is his appetite for learning.

The mistaken notion that we have already arrived is the height of immaturity; maturity is the recognition that we haven't. Humility in life as well as before the Lord is the indispensable virtue of a teachable spirit in the life of a good leader. Being teachable reflects the realization that my knowledge is still incomplete.

Genuine humility creates a thirst for the wisdom of the Lord. Without such a "faith filter," no one is prepared to distinguish the ideas of the world from the truth of God.

The psalmist sang that God "guides the humble in what is right and teaches them his way" (Psalm 25:9, *NIV*).

The prophet Isaiah preached that God esteems the one who is humble and contrite in spirit, and who trembles at His Word (see Isaiah 66:2, *NIV*).

Monica Baldwin's statement about humility has haunted me since I first read it: "What makes humility so desirous is the marvelous thing it does to us; it creates in us the capacity for the closest possible intimacy with God."

The most autobiographical statement Jesus made was His description of Himself as humble and gentle of heart (see Matthew 11:29). In that same passage He used the metaphor of the yoke to speak about the need for His disciples to learn from Him. Spurgeon said it so well many years ago: Jesus "is His own best lesson."

Lord, may we offer ourselves to You in each and every circumstance. We ask You to teach and shape us more and more into the image of Christ. May we have the mind of Christ and model His life.

Three Questions to Think About

1. In what ways am I closed-minded?
2. How friendly am I with my ignorance?
3. Who is encouraging me to be more teachable?

One Line to Remember

A leader makes friends with his or her ignorance.

Scripture to Hide in Your Heart

Is not wisdom found among the aged? Does not long life bring understanding? (Job 12:12).

45

THE EXCELLENT COMMUNICATOR

Fred's Observation

Good communication is more than presence, delivery or even content. A truly great communicator understands three important principles.

First, he or she understands that it is crucial to have the spirit of communication. The speaker should be motivated to *express*, not *impress*. My friend Dr. Jim Cain accepted an invitation to speak in front of 2,000 key executives about stress. He was preceded at the podium by a renowned cardiologist and a famous psychiatrist who got caught in the competition of impressing each other. When Dr. Cain spoke, he used a simple analogy to describe what the audience needed to know. This distinguished Mayo Clinic physician understood the spirit of communication. He expressed, not impressed.

Second, great communicators understand that they should avoid registering shock. When a person shows shock, it automatically says to the other individual that their value systems are obviously in conflict, and unpolluted communication immediately becomes impossible. Clearly, teenagers use the shock factor as a way to avoid communication entirely. Wise parents listen while keeping physical and mental control—"never let them see you sweat."

Third, good communicators display interest, not curiosity. Interest through listening and skillful questioning opens understanding. Each of us wants to feel that another is sincerely interested, but none of us wants to be the target of curiosity. I see the difference this way: Interest gives you information for the other person's benefit; curiosity is helpful simply for you. Let me give you an example. I was on the phone with a young woman who was obviously crying. A curious question would have been, "Why are you crying?" An interested question begins with asking permission, "Do you want to tell me why you are crying?" Interest, not curiosity, opens a door.

A true communicator has a message and a mandate. An adept communicator knows that energy, passion, skillfulness and experience follow the gift that is used wisely and well.

Reflection: Mac Brunson

Senior Pastor, First Baptist Church, Jacksonville, Florida

Without sounding gratuitous, this is the genius of Fred Smith. There are three principles here that are critical to every good communicator, but only one of those deals with speaking. The other two principles deal with our listening and how we listen. Effective communication is only one-third what we say and two-thirds how we have connected with those to whom we are speaking. How many times can you remember your mother saying, "Listen twice as much as you speak"?

When you listen, you make a connection. How you listen, as Fred has suggested, impacts your communication. It is critical to listen to those to whom you are going to communicate. How you listen to them either builds a bridge or erects a wall.

As a pastor, whenever I preach, I know that my listeners are people who are one decision away from moral, financial, marital or personal ruin. The others are considering options that will follow them the rest of their lives. The question is not *Are they listening?* but *Have I earned the right to be heard in order to effectively communicate God's Word?* Only then has communication taken place.

Fred also speaks of the spirit of communication. My wife always tells me, "Speak to the heart and not the head." What she is saying is what Fred has stated—don't try to impress others, but speak to their needs. Someone once said, "It is impossible to impress them with Jesus and yourself at the same time."

Three Questions to Think About

1. When am I guilty of impressing, not expressing?
2. What steps can I take to develop my message and mandate?
3. How do I move toward interest and away from curiosity?

One Line to Remember

Good communication is more than presence, delivery or even content.

Scripture to Hide in Your Heart

Let every person be quick to listen, slow to speak, slow to anger. (James 1:19).

46

MOTIVATING THROUGH MANDATES

Fred's Observation

U.S. diplomat Adolph A. Berle, writing about power, said that a leader should always operate from a mandate and that both the leader and the people must hold to it. Great politicians have long found this true. For example, President Franklin D. Roosevelt listed four fears we should overcome. Dictators have always presented their mandate as formed for the good of the people; the mandate then becomes the great motivating reality.

Max DePree, author and CEO, made current reality his mandate when he said, "The chief responsibility of any CEO is to define reality for the organization." Mr. John D. Rockefeller of Chase Manhattan chose vision. He thought that the chief responsibility of a leader is to define vision for the organization. In other words, the attainable potential becomes the target. It mandates and defines the ultimate aim of the organization.

A clear mandate also becomes a correct way of evaluating progress. The great executives I have known choose to lead in a way that sacrifices their egos *to* the organization rather than satisfying it *from* the organization.

Selecting a proper mandate requires objective integrity. I have found it very profitable to associate with people who think with exceptional clarity. One such friend and advisor lives in Colorado. I remember describing a problem to him. He asked about my options, and I confidently told him that I had three.

"Tell me about them," he said.

He listened as I described each of them and then pointedly replied, "You don't have three options–you have one option and two wishes."

Sometimes an outside, objective, but friendly view can be invaluable. Entrusting the integrity of the mandate to leadership means they are trustworthy. The acceptance of a mandate by leadership accents responsibility rather than rights. Rights generally clash and separate. Responsibilities overlap and form a bond. The mandate calls the organization to accountability–starting at the top.

Reflection: Sarah Sumner

Professor of Theology and Ministry,
Special Assistant to the Dean for Strategic Development,
Haggard Graduate School of Theology
Teaching Pastor, New Song Church, San Dimas, California

In practical terms, to "define reality" is to frame other people's perspectives. It's to call their attention to an ongoing problem that the mandate promises to solve. Thus with every call to the mandate, the leader must reiterate the problem that the mandate resolves. Too often leaders sell the mandate prematurely. They try to sell the mandate by itself. They forget that it's the problem that makes the mandate meaningful. So when a leader is casting a vision, the onus is on the leader first to groan about the problem and then to paint a picture of what reality would be like if everyone would champion the mandate.

Indeed, no leader can lead effectively without a clear mandate, and yet establishing a mandate is not enough. In order for the leader to stay the course long-term, the leader has to cultivate personal character. It's the character of the leader that determines whether or not the leader will be true to the mandate.

There are three main traps that leaders are most likely to fall into: cynicism, people-pleasing and image management.

Cynicism arises when a leader loses faith in the people who are entrusted with the mandate. The antidote to cynicism is to celebrate all the things that people on the team do right and forgive them for what they do wrong.

By contrast, people pleasing results from fear. When the leader becomes afraid of other people's anger, the leader loses sight of the mandate. The antidote to people pleasing is to set wise emotional boundaries in relationships so that the leader can love the people instead of fearing them.

Finally, image management takes over when a leader begins to care more about appearances than reality. Deceitfulness drives image management. Thus the antidote to image management is honesty. Truth sets leaders free to champion the mandate long-term.

Three Questions to Think About

1. What is my operating mandate?
2. How am I properly controlling my ego?
3. How clearly am I defining reality for others around me?

One Line to Remember

The acceptance of a mandate by leadership accents responsibility rather than rights.

Scripture to Hide in Your Heart

Hold to the standard of sound words that you heard from me and do so with the faith and love that are in Christ Jesus (2 Timothy 1:13).

47

STRETCHING THE WHEELBASE

Fred's Observation

So many people live their emotional life like a yo-yo, going from high to low and back again. A Sufi parable alleges that a powerful king challenged his wise men to create a ring for him that would bring stability to his reign. The sages put their heads together and came back with a gold ring engraved with the phrase "This too shall pass." We need to realize that this motto applies to all of us as well.

As we mature, we learn to lengthen our emotional wheelbase. We take the bumps with less jolting. This realization brings equilibrium to our life. I find pessimists extrapolate the bad too far into life and the optimists extrapolate good too far. Time and opportunity change conditions so that Smith's maxim says, "Extrapolate objectively."

Sometimes we feel like a sailor on a storm-tossed ship, accepting both the waves and the security of the ship like a sailor does. Other times our life makes us feel like a soldier on terra firma. We soon realize that we are no safer as a soldier than as a sailor—there just aren't any waves washing over us when we're on dry land! Whatever our condition, we need to keep in focus what we are trying to accomplish. An aim without a target is worthless.

Part of keeping focus is to keep the machinery well oiled. To me this means developing a sense of humor. I see some people running with excessive heat who are doing damage to the machine simply because they don't have that little shot of oil to lubricate and dissipate the heat. There is no better oil than a sense of humor.

Yo-yos are fun for children, but a yo-yo life makes even the most sure-footed adult seasick.

Reflection: Larry Mercer

President, Washington Bible College/Capital Bible Seminary/ Equip Institute, Washington, D.C.

In a recent moment off-stage from pastoral or professional leadership, my teenaged daughter exclaimed, "Dad, you are crazy!" It was one of our most memorable moments together. Her spontaneous diagnosis of my temporary "craziness" felt like a wonderful affirmation of my humanity and it was medicine for my spirit. Let me explain.

We had just finished sharing a burst of laughter after an instance when I shed any semblance of pastoral or professional demeanor and got lost in a moment of parental fun. Moments of fun and healthy release are not only a nice counterweight to the pressures from life and ministry, but they can also save our lives. In that moment I could give personal testimony to the claims of modern research that laughter reduces dangerous hormones, lowers blood pressure and decreases stress. It felt good.

No wonder the writer of Proverbs recognized the healing power of laughter when he noted, "A cheerful heart brings good healing, but a crushed spirit dries up the bones" (Proverbs 17:22).

Fred's words are great incentives to protect our spirits from being broken by the weight of service without windows of laughter. When I think of a life without laughter, I can't help but think of the image of a rubber band under constant tension. I am challenged to keep the machine of life well oiled with minutes of enjoyment, knowing that God is able to give the gift of enjoyment described in Ecclesiastes 5:19-20: "Moreover, when God gives any man wealth and possessions, and enables him to enjoy them, to accept his lot and be happy in his work—this is a gift of God. He seldom reflects on the days of his life, because God keeps him occupied with gladness of heart" (*NIV*).

Three Questions to Think About

1. How do I create a yo-yo effect in my life?
2. Do I honestly extrapolate objectively?
3. What makes me stop and laugh?

One Line to Remember

As we mature, we learn to lengthen our emotional wheelbase.

Scripture to Hide in Your Heart

At that time we laughed loudly and shouted for joy (Psalm 126:2).

48

KEEPING CALM

Fred's Observation

Most of us view success as fame, accomplishment and acquisition. Our society has chosen personality over character. Christian success must be built, instead, on character and not personality—or even skill. The measurement of success is simply the ratio of talents used to talents received. Success involves having a great sense of responsibility and a love for God and other people. Out of this will flow a tremendous use of our talents. Success, for a Christian, is built on character.

The great qualities in life involved in a person's character are wisdom, integrity, honesty, loyalty, faith, forgiveness and love. *The Everyday Bible* gives an interesting translation of Psalm 131:1, which says, "Lord, my heart is not proud. I do not look down on others. I do not do great things and I cannot do miracles. But I am calm and quiet." How can we claim Christian success unless our hearts are calm and quiet?

I was doing a series of television programs with well-known athletes associated with former All-Pro Bill Glass's prison ministry. At lunch with Craig Morton and "Mean" Joe Green, I asked, "What is a quarterback's most important quality?"

Joe answered, "He is relaxed in the pocket. I don't mean asleep but in control."

Panic is never a good option.

Thomas Kelly, the eminent Quaker philosopher, said that inside each person there should be a quiet center that nothing can disturb. The great Catholic mystics continually talked of the throne of God, which is in the innermost part of our heart, where no storm, tribulation or temptation can disturb us. Scripture says, "Greater is he that controls his spirit than he who takes a city" (see Proverbs 16:32). Obviously our condition is more valuable than our accomplishment. Our greatest success is the condition of a quiet and peaceful heart.

Reflection: John Temple

President/CEO (Retired), Guideposts, Incorporated

When I first read Fred's statement that our society has chosen personality over character, I smiled, because I couldn't agree more. Look at Terrell Owens of the Dallas Cowboys—all personality, no character.

But I've never liked the idea that if I'm to be a success as a Christian and a CEO, I must be calm and quiet. To me, "calm" means placid, weak. It doesn't speak to my chaotic, active, dynamic life. I'm a CEO; I fly a plane. I want action, excitement—not calm or quiet.

As I thought more about Fred's ideas, however, I thought about a football quarterback, with the pocket breaking down and huge linemen trying to disrupt his efforts. I realized that the quarterback works best when he is calm, focused, poised, controlled. Now I was beginning to see what Fred meant.

Being cool under pressure is certainly an attribute of effective leadership. Henry Kissinger, at the death of former President Gerald Ford, said that "he [Ford] took over at perhaps the most perilous moment of domestic crisis . . . but he moved with calm and surefootedness."[1]

I understand Fred's use of "calm." To be a true leader, I must have a calm and confident core that strengthens me and all those around me.

Three Questions to Think About

1. Where do I find my quiet core?
2. What is troubling my spirit?
3. How do I regain my equilibrium?

One Line to Remember

Our greatest success is the condition of a quiet and peaceful heart.

Scripture to Hide in Your Heart

The words of the wise are heard in quiet, more than the shouting of a ruler is heard among fools (Ecclesiastes 9:17).

Note

1. Henry Kissinger, "In Memoriam: Recollections of the public and private Gerald Ford," *Newsweek*, January 8, 2007. http://207.46.245.33/id/16409199/site/newsweek/ (accessed April 2007).

49

HEAVEN'S TUG

Fred's Observation

Now that Mary Alice is in heaven, we have a divine magnet—our hearts are drawn to heaven. Thanksgiving 2005 was the first holiday that the family had gathered together since her remembrance service. We all took turns expressing gratitude for her life and continuing influence in the family. It was clear that though absent, she was still very present among us. Our grandchildren regret that their children will not grow up knowing "Grandmother."

As we went around the room, my six-year-old great-grandson Andrew was asked what he was thankful for. "That Grandmother loved me so much," was his instant and heartfelt answer.

Mary Alice's death made us very conscious of Psalm 23: "When we walk through the valley we will have no fear." This was fortified by Dr. Ramesh Richard's conversation with the funeral director at the gravesite. He asked him, "Can you tell the difference between families of faith and nonfaith?"

The funeral home official replied, "In about two minutes."

We were pleased that so many commented that the service honored Mary Alice and glorified God. Of course, we grieve, but "not as those without hope."

Her death makes eternity more immediate—heaven and hell are more real. It has increased the intensity of my intercessory prayer for unbelieving friends. It has revealed to me the role that we are meant to play in each other's lives. A lifelong friend called and said, "Your wife was a fine Christian lady, and without the Christian witness of you two, I don't know where I would be." While it is the Holy Spirit that brings others to Christ, we are permitted the privilege of introducing them both through our life and our word.

Our magnet draws us heavenward, but our faith keeps us firmly planted on the earth doing the work that He has given us to do. I rest assured that I will see again this woman of faith—this true lady.

Reflection: Jeff Horch

Grandson, Fred Smith, Sr. and Son of Brenda A. Smith
Multi-media Producer

Speaking at a memorial service is normally a somber moment, but representing the grandchildren at my grandmother's service was one of my greatest joys. To share with the audience of family and friends about a woman I admired and loved was a unique privilege that I will never forget. On that cold November day, I spoke of two of the qualities that defined my grandmother as a "lady." Right now, I would like to focus on just the first quality: dignity.

When we think of the word "dignity," we might think of royalty or of those who keep themselves separate from things "undignified." But dignity is actually a great biblical quality. It's the idea of understanding that you have worth and value that comes from being created in the image of God. I always believed my grandmother had this innate sense of her worth, so she carried herself with dignity.

But even greater is the fact that she brought dignity to others. She continued to remind her grandchildren of their value and worth. I know as her grandson that when I saw her love me, care for me and believe in me, I couldn't help but think (even as a young boy) that I must be special. I believed from an early age that I must have value because of the way my grandmother loved me. She was a woman who built up and encouraged her grandchildren by continually reminding us of the person she saw in us. It is powerful to view our lives through the eyes of a grandmother.

Today, in many ways, I know that who I am is because of who she saw in me.

Three Questions to Think About

1. If I died today, how would I be remembered?
2. Who is a great encourager in my life?
3. How often do I pray for the salvation of unbelievers?

One Line to Remember

Our magnet draws us heavenward, but our faith keeps us firmly planted on the earth doing the work that He has given us to do.

Scripture to Hide in Your Heart

Her children rise up and call her blessed, her husband also praises her (Proverbs 31:28).

50

ORGANIZING FOR RESULTS

Fred's Observation

Establishing a mandate helps us to define the reality of our task and to lead with integrity. Leaders need to ask, "Why are we operating? What are we about? What are we dedicated to?" Once these questions have been addressed and consensus around the answers is developed, a leader has a mandate. This mandate will be the foundation upon which programs can be developed, recruitment of additional leaders can begin, an organizational culture can be established, and then an understanding of what to do and what not to do can occur.

One critical function of a mandate is that it separates loyalty to the leader from loyalty to the cause. The leader has to say, "I am subservient to the mandate." A good leader knows that the organization isn't there to make him or her happy, nor to serve him or her. It is there to fulfill the mandate. If the leader fails in doing that, he or she should be fired.

I once spoke with 10 pastors who have PhDs. One asked, "How can I get my church to do my program?"

I responded by asking him, "Did you found the church?" His answer was a clear no. I then asked him, "If you got a better offer, would you leave?" His answer again was clear—yes. "Then what right do you have to call it 'my' church?" I said. "The church isn't a personal possession."

While the leader is responsible for the initiation of the mandate, he or she has to build a consensus for it among the people. First, all must buy into the mandate; second, all must be willing to dedicate themselves to carrying it out. Christ gave us His mandate and empowered His disciples to begin 2,000 years of carrying it out!

Reflection: Ben Haden

President, Ben Haden Evangelical Association, Inc.

In the newspaper business, I was CEO of a corporation that published a Republican morning paper, a Democratic afternoon paper and an Independent Sunday paper. The mandate was to *tell the factual truth*, with opinion or bias restricted to editorials and choice of syndicated columnists. Eventually all three papers became independent, requiring no change in staff, style or news—because the mandate had been observed.

When Fred cites a pastor and a church, he immediately focuses on the mandate. How right he is! The average church would probably appoint a committee.

After entering the pastorate from business, I always concentrated on the same mandate in the two churches (in Miami and Chattanooga) I served: "Our business is people. Our purpose is Jesus Christ."

Consistent with that mandate, it has been my habit to hire staff pastors from different denominations, different backgrounds and different seminaries. Though both churches were *denominational*, the stated approach was always *nondenominational*. Why? Because our mandate was *people*—all kinds of people from all kinds of backgrounds and denominations.

The purpose remained *Jesus Christ*. To avoid seeking personal loyalty above loyalty to the mandate, I never hired a classmate or anyone else from my seminary.

Since our mandate was *people*, all staff members counseled, led to Christ, presided, preached and taught. Attendance did not vary when different staff members led a service. Titles were not used. Each minister was listed as "pastor"—not "associate" or "assistant." Consistent with the mandate, members always prayed for *our pastors*. This approach caused both workload and credit to be divided among the pastors.

In my opinion, the major pitfall in the pastorate is to have a mandate of denominationalism, a certain theology, a certain style. Nothing should interfere with our mandate from Christ to love Him, love our neighbors, and fulfill the Great Commission.

Three Questions to Think About

1. How can I describe my professional and personal mandates?
2. To what am I truly loyal?
3. What is the value of truth in my daily life?

One Line to Remember

Establishing a mandate helps us to define the reality of our task and to lead with integrity.

Scripture to Hide in Your Heart

I heard the voice of the sovereign master say, "Whom will I send? Who will go on our behalf?" I answered, "Here am I, send me!" (Isaiah 6:8).

51

BUILDING BLOCKS FOR SUCCESSFUL LIVING

Fred's Observation

Good habits help to develop good character. When I was in business, I worked with an executive who started as a poor boy, selling vegetables from his garden and wagon on the streets of New York. After finishing public school, he got his degree in accounting at night. He joined the corporation and later he became executive vice president of a major company.

I once asked him to what he attributed his success. He replied, "Several things, but mainly my good work habits. I don't always use them, but I've got them." I laughed and said, "I've got good habits too, but like you, I don't always use them." He said sharply, "You misunderstood. When I want to work, I don't use my habits, but when I don't want to work, I *have* to use them."

Good habits not only bring us success; they also save us time. Once I told my friend Mr. Jarman that I was a person of few habits. He replied, "You must waste a lot of time."

Habits should always be kept current in order to be effective. As our responsibilities change, so should some of our habits. Therefore it is important to occasionally reassess our habits to be sure they are still needed and effective. Here are four that seem to be essential at all times:

1. Punctuality
2. Truthfulness
3. Perseverance
4. Willingness to accept responsibility

Make no excuses and give yourself no free passes, because habits are the first step in a critical process. Habits become reflexes, which become automatic responses, which then become a lifestyle. It is important not to make exceptions to good habits. Bad habits can become ingrained just as good ones can, so the decision to monitor the development of positive habits is key in personal development.

An automatic pilot system erected on good habits enables us to say "I will" when "I won't" seems a lot more natural.

Reflection: Haley Smith

Granddaughter of Fred Smith, Sr. and Daughter of Fred Smith, Jr. and Carol W. Smith
2007 Graduate of Baylor University

I laughed when I read my grandfather's weekly thought. The only positive habit that I could think of was that I habitually check my email. (Too bad I haven't formed the habit of immediately responding to any of them.) Years ago I developed the "gift of procrastination," and it has gradually strengthened during my time at Baylor.

During an internship at Mission Waco, my friend Laura and I were responsible for creating the organizational newsletter. We delayed designing the layout until the weekend before it was due, knowing it would only take a few hours at most to complete. Well, of course we were wrong—and it took us 25 hours to design the newsletter. We literally finished the newsletter about one hour before it was due!

After thinking about what Grandfather wrote, I realize that procrastinating on this project had deeper consequences than just causing some unneeded stress. In putting off the newsletter, I was disrespectful to my boss and the organization—and I fed a habit that is in no way positive or productive. I put off this project because it wasn't one of my top interests, yet it was still one of my responsibilities.

When I work with the kids at Mission Waco, I am never late and strive to make their happiness my top priority. I do this because I am passionate about their lives and need no habits to help me complete my work with them. This is a selfish way to live. If I have surrendered my life to Christ, why should I be able to choose what is important and necessary? I cannot fully complete and fulfill the things that I am passionate about without also being responsible for tasks that are not always fun and interesting to me.

It is the formation of productive habits that will ultimately help to achieve the larger picture for my life.

Three Questions to Think About

1. What are some of my best habits?
2. In what areas have I lacked accomplishment due to bad habits?
3. Are there habits that I no longer need?

One Line to Remember

It is important not to make exceptions to good habits.

Scripture to Hide in Your Heart

But the one who peers into the perfect law of liberty and fixes his attention there, and does not become a forgetful listener but one who lives it out—he will be blessed in what he does (James 1:25).

52

ROCK-SOLID CHARACTER

Fred's Observation

I received a question through the "Ask Fred" column on www.breakfastwithfred.com that intrigued me greatly: "What do you think are the three dominant traits of a good character?" Three would be very easy to name, but as I thought about it more deeply, I realized that it would require at least seven traits for the character to be truly strong.

First, a *love of truth.* A total desire for truth is almost a divine quality because Christ alone is truth. By our nature we like to be selective with truth, keeping fantasies that are pleasant to us.

Second, *objectivity.* This is probably the most difficult to consistently maintain. We must go through a refining process, smelting out our prejudices, biases and perceived self-interests.

Third, *courage.* It is always in opposition to a temptation. The primary emphasis here is the courage of self-realization, accepting who we are with both our weaknesses and our strengths.

Fouth, *perseverance.* This is often the dominant characteristic of great accomplishment. For example, Thomas A. Edison reportedly had 10,000 failures along with his noteworthy achievements.

Fifth, *Stewardship.* The realization of our stewardship rather than our ownership gives us a correct view of life.

Stewardship is responsibility; ownership is rights.

Sixth, *humility*. It is not denying the power we have, but admitting it comes through us and not from us.

Seventh, *gratitude*. Scientifically, it has been shown to be the healthiest of all emotions, yet one of the most fragile. True gratitude is being thankful that someone else has done for you what you couldn't do for yourself.

The vitality of each trait is important. Each must carry its full weight in the formation of character. Any trait that becomes weakened presages a break in character. Remember that old saying that a chain is only as strong as its weakest link? Character is no different.

Reflection: Brenda A. Smith

Daughter of Fred Smith, Sr.
President, BWF Project, Incorporated

"They have character in their face—I like them." My mom's assessment was usually swift and almost always final. She read faces by reading *behind* the face. Ignoring her evaluation inevitably led to regret. Mom didn't analyze the seven traits of a solid character as Dad did—she simply knew good character when she saw it!

"Your Dad always makes me think," my mom told me. He makes me think as well. He makes me look at the woman I am and carefully measure how much I love truth or hold things lightly as a steward and not an owner. His incisive definition of humility makes me look at my God-given gifts differently.

But gratitude is the showstopper. When Dad quotes Hans Selye's research on gratitude, it pierces my heart: "It is the most fragile of all emotions." The apostle Paul tells us "in everything give thanks" (1 Thessalonians 5:18). Ouch!

But Dad is right—the ungrateful heart is hollow because it has no space for acknowledging the gifts of others. In the care-giving process, I have grown weary many times. Too often grumpiness has outpaced grace, and I respond out of ingratitude rather than in gratitude.

Anne, my college roommate, was told as a child to eat her vegetables because "it builds character." In third grade she announced to her mom that pea eating was over because she had all the character she needed and wanted. How well I understand that! However, Dad reminds me that a woman of character reflects a refined heart that only Jesus gives. All the jolly green giants and a lifetime of leafy green vegetables cannot provide what God has prepared for us before the world began. As we grow to look more like Jesus, we understand that character is merely a reflection of the God who loves us.

Three Questions to Think About

1. Which one of these traits is my strongest?
2. Which of these traits is my weakest?
3. What am I doing to build character in others?

One Line to Remember

True gratitude is being thankful that someone else has done for you what you couldn't do for yourself.

Scripture to Hide in Your Heart

Look, the one whose desires are not upright will faint from exhaustion, but the person of integrity will live because of his faithfulness (Habakkuk 2:4).

CONTRIBUTORS

MARK BAILEY
Fred and Mark have a mutual respect for Dallas Theological Seminary. Their motto of "Preach the Word" clearly articulates their common interest in the honest proclamation of the gospel.

JIM BECKETT
Jim credits Fred with changing his business life through wise mentoring and friendship. Jim hosts a birthday party for Fred twice a year—"just in case."

KEN BLANCHARD
Ken and Fred share a common desire to help others to use their gifts effectively. They impact others for good through their speaking and writing.

JILL BRISCOE
Fred and Jill served on the Christianity Today Inter-national board together. He and her husband, Stuart, have been friends for years. Fred regards Jill's influence on women throughout the world as remarkable.

STEVE BROWN
Fred enjoys thinking about ideas to use on and with his "iron sharpens iron" buddy, Steve Brown. A friend for decades, they enjoy humor, honesty and mental stimulation.

MAC BRUNSON
Mac and Fred share a common heritage, common friends and a common goal of communicating truth with impact and influence.

HOWARD E. BUTT, JR.
Fred's relationship with Howard began in the 1950s at Baylor University when Fred spoke at "Religious Emphasis Weeks." He and Howard have labored together in Christian laywork for 50 years.

DONALD CAMPBELL
Don and Fred love truth and knowledge. They share a common bond through their mutual friendship with Ray Stedman.

BOB DEFFINBAUGH
Bob rides shotgun at the Fred in the Bed sessions. "He is the clearest, finest Bible student I know—we make a great team," says Fred. A family friend for decades, Bob serves as a perfect straight man for Fred's humor.

RICHARD ALLEN FARMER
Richard and Fred are recent friends. Each of them are motivated by ideas, music and reading.

H. JOHANNA FISHER
Johanna's friendship with Fred began through connections with KCBI, a local Christian radio station in Dallas, Texas. Now a family friend, she continues to quote Fred Smith.

JOHN GILLESPIE
Fred met John when he was given the annual Roaring Lambs Hall of Fame award for an outstanding Christian in business. John saw the potential for Fred to be a "Paul to many Timothys" and took Fred's principles and applied them to real life.

BILL GLASS
"Bill is a man sold out for the gospel of Christ," says Fred of Bill. As a college student, Bill found in Fred the qualities of a lifetime mentor.

RON GLOSSER
Fred and Ron have a friendship of service and genuine admiration in which they focus on how best to do the work of Christ. Fred refers to Ron as the man with the "world's best network."

BEN HADEN
Fred states, "When Ben says, 'Jesus is my best friend,' I know he means it—and most don't." Ben and Fred have a deep friendship, based on speaking the truth, and mutually mentor each other.

JOHN EDMUND HAGGAI
John and Fred met in the early days of the Christian lay movement and both see the need for intellectual courage. John views Fred as a wisdom figure for this generation.

T. GEORGE HARRIS

George and Fred's relationship is one of intellectual eagerness. The breadth of George's experience and knowledge often lights Fred's mental fires.

EVELYN HINDS

Evelyn and her husband, Rob, are faithful members of the conversational open house that meets each week at Fred's house. She coined the phrase "Fred in the Bed" to describe the Saturday morning group meetings around Fred's bed.

VICKI HITZGES

Vicki's father, Haddon Robinson, is a close personal friend. Fred introduces Vicki as "the fastest growing professional woman speaker in America."

JEFF HORCH

Fred's usual parting remark to his grandson Jeff is, "Be a blessing, Jeff–I'm proud of you."

HENRY HORRELL

Henry is Fred's longest living friend. They grew up in north Nashville with a dream to grow and become something. Fred and Mary Alice served as witnesses in at Henry's wedding nearly 70 years ago.

MAX HULSE

"Did you know Max plays the harmonica?" Fred will ask before asking Max to play something for the group. Fred respects Max's ability to combine his business, artistic and Christian interests.

CHARLIE "TREMENDOUS" JONES

Fred says that "Charlie is a man who wastes no time on frivolous matters." Charlie and Fred shared a speaking platform for years, and Charlie has singlehandedly made *You and Your Network* a national bestseller.

JAY KESLER

Jay was introduced to Fred through his work with Youth for Christ. Together, they served on boards, developing great rapport. "Jay is a man with a heart for America's young people," Fred once remarked.

GARRY D. KINDER
Garry's work in business and ministry has been influenced by Fred's principles and thinking. Their joint ministry board work allows them to encourage young leaders.

JACK KINDER
Jack and Fred enjoy communication, leadership and motivation. Jack and his brother Garry operate their business on many of the principles they received from Fred.

VERDELL DAVIS KREISHER
Fred has watched Verdell's influence grow through her counseling, writing and speaking. She considers him a mentor and friend.

SETH C. MACON
Fred and Seth's lifetime friendship began when Fred spoke to Seth's insurance company. "Seth is a man without guile," Fred says.

JOHN MAXWELL
John has said that Fred's *Learning to Lead* is one of the best books written on leadership. Their friendship is based on mutual respect and a love for learning.

PETER MCNALLY
Peter began his mentoring relationship with Fred during one of the many "breakfasts with Fred." Peter initiated the AM/PM group so called because it met in the morning (A.M.) and was hosted by Peter McNally (P.M.)—an assembling of high achievers mentored by Fred.

CURTIS MEADOWS
Fred's friendship with Curtis began when Fred substituted for Jim Smith, a lifelong teacher, at Highland Park Presbyterian Church in Dallas, Texas. Fred enjoys Curtis's expertise in nonprofit leadership and his love of music.

LARRY MERCER
Larry leads a community of young men and women seeking wisdom and truth. Fred's writings and life strongly influence his work.

JACK MODESETT, JR.
Fred says that Jack, a friend and mentoree since the 1970s, has "the finest mental organ of any man I know." Conversations between the two play like two jazz musicians. Jack was the first recipient of CTI's Fred Smith Leadership Award.

HAROLD MYRA
Harold and Fred's friendship began with Youth for Christ. Fred speaks of Harold as one who is an example of "truly fine executive leadership."

GREG NOLAND
Fred proudly notes that grandson Greg is the first member of the family to receive a doctorate degree.

MARY HELEN NOLAND
Mary Helen is a beloved daughter of Fred who brings joy and pride to his heart. "It makes me glad to hear about the difference her life makes," he says.

RUTH STAFFORD PEALE
Ruth's husband, Norman Vincent Peale, had a great impact on Fred's early speaking. In later years, his friendship with the Peale organization allowed him to appreciate the leadership of this graceful woman.

JOY LYNN HAILEY REED
Joy Lynn and Fred met in Zig Ziglar's Sunday School class. She soon joined the "Fred in the Bed" group, bringing her brightness and intellectual thirst to the meetings.

RAMESH RICHARD
Fred says that Ramesh "is my personal theologian." Ramesh is a faithful friend and respected mentoree.

HADDON ROBINSON
"*Time* magazine lists Haddon as one of the top 10 preachers in America," is how Fred usually introduces Haddon. The two have had a long and fruitful friendship.

RANDY SAMELSON
Fred says that Randy "is probably my most astute mentoree." Fred values Randy's thinking, integrity and his commitment to serving well.

DONNA SKELL
Donna considers herself a devoted mentoree of Fred's. He often asks her to talk about her love for evangelism and eagerness to see others come to faith.

BRENDA A. SMITH
"She likes to think of herself as my cruise director," says Fred. "Grateful daughter" and "privileged care manager" also describe her.

FRED SMITH
Fred Sr. often remarks, "I wish every man had a relationship with his son like I have with Fred."

HALEY SMITH
This lively and lovely young woman is Fred's graceful granddaughter. "Haley always puts a smile on my face," says Fred.

SARAH SUMNER
Sarah is a mentoree-at-a-distance, having never met Fred, and his principle-based thinking and writing have influenced her own academic work. She represents the new generation of thinkers who benefit from his writing and the website.

JOHN TEMPLE
Fred states that "John is a great executive—he knows business, he knows people, and he knows how to take action." Fred and John became acquainted through Fred's relationship with the Guideposts organization.

MARGARITA C. TREVIÑO
Fred's writings have had an influence on Margarita. Her impact on students and the academic community displays her leadership.

JACK TURPIN

Fred often speaks of Jack as a "man of vision, hard work, and genuine love for his family." The two met monthly for breakfasts and mentoring sessions when Jack was building his business.

PAT WILLIAMS

Pat uses Fred's wisdom as he leads his organization and his family. He points to the principle-based thinking he received from Fred as being very influential in his life.

PHILIP YANCEY

Fred first met Philip through Youth for Christ International. Fred speaks of him as one of the truly great Christian writers.

ZIG ZIGLAR

Zig often calls Fred one of the wisest men he has ever known. He proudly calls him a mentor and friend.